When the Kings Come Marching In

ISAIAH AND THE NEW JERUSALEM

Richard J. Mouw

GRAND RAPIDS, MICHIGAN
WILLIAM B. EERDMANS PUBLISHING COMPANY

Library of Congress Cataloging in Publication Data

Mouw, Richard J.
      When the kings come marching in.

      1. Bible.   O.T.   Isaiah LX—Criticism, interpretation,
etc.   2. Christianity and culture.   I. Title.
BS1515.2.M68   224′.106   83-8933
ISBN 0-8028-1935-4

The Scripture quotations in this publication are from the Revised Standard Version of the Bible, copyrighted 1946, 1952, © 1971, 1973 by the Division of Christian Education of the National Council of the Churches of Christ in the U.S.A., and used by permission.

Contents

Preface

When I was invited a few years ago to give a series of Bible-study type lectures at Bethel College in North Newton, Kansas, my hosts encouraged me to choose a theme that would be considered provocative on an Anabaptist campus. I chose to organize my lectures around what I take to be the "transformation of culture" emphasis in Isaiah 60. My Mennonite hearers, while gracious and receptive, were not uniformly "non-resistant" in their responses to what I had to say. I came away from that stimulating encounter with a new appreciation for the complexities of the theme which I had been developing.

Since then I have tried out the revised version of my thoughts on three audiences: those at Regent College and Fuller Theological Seminary, and the Woodbury (Pa.) congregation of the Church of the Brethren. In each case I gained much from the dialogue which took place. I have also benefitted greatly from the critical comments of several colleagues— John Cooper, David Lyon, George Marsden, and Calvin Van Reken—who read an earlier draft of this manuscript.

Most of my work on this little book took place at Juniata College in Huntingdon, Pennsylvania, where I spent the 1980-81 academic year as the J. Omar Good Visiting Professor of Evangelical Christianity. I am grateful to that campus community for providing me with a pleasant and stimulating environment in which to work. I am especially indebted to Mrs. Anne Edgin, my secretary at Juniata, for her skillful labors on the manuscript. I also benefitted from many phone conversations during that year with Jon Pott of Eerdmans, who offered guidance and encouragement for this project.

While writing this book I re-read *Pilgrim's Progress*, John Bunyan's classic treatment of the Christian's difficult journey toward the Gates of Light. For me, one of the saddest features of that book is Bunyan's portrayal of the pilgrim as having left behind his wife and children in his quest for the Celestial City—a tragedy which Bunyan only partly remedies by having the pilgrim's family pursue the same path in the second part of the allegory. In reflecting upon the theme of the Holy City, I have been constantly aware of the immeasurable advantage over Bunyan's pilgrim which I enjoy. To Phyllis and Dirk, for all that they have given me on the journey thus far, I offer my deepest gratitude.

Introduction

As a Christian philosopher teaching at a Christian liberal arts college, I am very interested in questions of "Christ and culture." These questions bear directly on the courses which I teach, and they come up regularly in discussions with students and former students who are struggling with vocation-oriented issues. The questions also appear as pressing challenges to me in my own attempts to be a Christian.

There are important disagreements among Christians over how we are to relate to culture. H. Richard Niebuhr's classic work, *Christ and Culture*, offers one way of classifying some of these long-standing disagreements. Some critics have suggested that Niebuhr's scheme is, in important respects, misleading. I have sympathies for this charge. But it is a fact nonetheless that genuine differences exist among Christians on the subject of cultural participation.

The differences of opinion become obvious when one examines systematic, scholarly discussions of "Christ and culture" themes. John Calvin portrays things quite differently than Martin Luther does; each of them, in turn, makes claims that stand in sharp contrast to the views of a Tertullian or a Saint Theresa or a Menno Simons. But the differences of opinion are not merely confined to the more theoretical kind of discussion. Recently I met a Mennonite lawyer. Since Mennonites have traditionally avoided the legal profession, I was interested in how this man had come to choose his profession. He gave a careful and sensitive explanation for his choice, but one that differed significantly from the rationales which I have heard offered by Calvinist and Lutheran and Roman Catholic lawyers. This man's explanation was a very Mennonite one, rooted in an Anabaptist perspective on Christ and culture.

It is dangerous, of course, to talk simply about "Christ and culture." Christ is a very complex person and culture is a very complex phenomenon. Neither Jesus nor culture is subject to a simple analysis, and it is unlikely that the relationship between them will be captured by easy formulas. Furthermore, the "Christ and culture" label is meant as shorthand for a number of interrelated issues, not the least being this question: How ought Christians to understand the proper patterns of their cultural involvement?

But Christians, too, are complex entities. We are complex people attempting to serve a complex Lord in a complex cultural environment. Because of these complexities, it is unlikely that any neat set of labels, such as the scheme set forth by Niebuhr, will accurately portray our actual views on cultural participation. No Christian really thinks that Christ is systematically "against" everything that can be labeled "culture"— nor that he is systematically "of" or "above" or "in tension with" or "transforming" such phenomena.

Niebuhr and others who have attempted to classify Christian perspectives on this subject have been aware of these complexities. Nonetheless, they have thought it helpful to locate certain patterns of thought, certain underlying motifs. I agree. Indeed, if I have to choose under pressure, I am rather quick to identify myself with those who long for the "transformation of culture." But I do feel under pressure when I must so identify myself without being able to introduce all of the necessary qualifications.

The meditations of this book are intended as a partial payment of a debt which I have incurred as a member of the "transformationalist" camp. We have sometimes—perhaps more often than we care to think—stated our case in too facile a fashion. In fact, "transformationalists" show a strong tendency to debate the issues on almost exclusively philosophical and systematic-theological grounds, while occasionally citing a few favorite biblical proof-texts—such as the so-called "cultural mandate" of Genesis 1—as a way of paying lip service to "the authority of Scripture." In these meditations I will attempt to remedy this defect by investigating some of the "Christ and culture" dialogue which occurs in the actual pages of the Bible.

My discussion here, then, is not intended primarily as a technical contribution, although I hope that it will not be without value for those who are interested in the technical questions. I will engage in a "Bible study," although I will not shrink from utilizing a "sermonic" mode of presentation.

The primary focus here will be on a single chapter in the Bible: Isaiah 60. I will, however, look at other passages, especially in Isaiah and the Book of Revelation. In Isaiah 60 the prophet envisions the future transformation of the city of Jerusalem, a portrayal of the Holy City which bears important similarities to John's vision in Revelation 21 and 22. Attention to these two visionary passages must be supplemented by a look at Hebrews 13:13-16, which applies the theme of the Holy City to the present patterns of our earthly pilgrimage.

The Bible deals with cultural attitudes on at least three levels. On the first level the biblical dialogue exhibits the virtue of historical concreteness. Here the biblical writers focus on very specific cultural entities, and on the attitudes which the believing community ought to exhibit toward them. God's people are given guidance regarding their dealings with specific kings and queens, with identifiable idols, with Lebanese wood and Corinthian meat.

A second level of generality is achieved when the references are not to specific cultural figures and artifacts but to nameable cultures. Here the people of God are often given principles or guidelines for dealing with this or that alien culture: "Drive out the Jebusites," "Do not imitate the Philistines," "Beware of the ways of the Syrians," "Flee Babylon."

But the biblical writers sometimes address issues on a third level of generality. Here they sometimes lump multiple cultures together into very broad categories, often intending a rather general and negative condemnation. Thus they speak of "the world," "this world," "this present age," or that which prevails "upon the earth."

This last set of terms, and other biblical equivalents, are the data out of which we often construct our general perspectives on "Christ and culture." "Christians must be different," someone will say. "We must not love this present world nor the things which are in it." "But," someone else will reply, "God still loves his world, and he is bringing his providential plan to fruition." "You are both correct, in a sense," a third party will say. "We must neither completely love this present age, nor completely withdraw from it. Rather. . . ." And the debate goes on.

But this kind of debate will produce very little fruit unless we examine the more specific levels of biblical discussion. In this regard Isaiah 60 is a very helpful passage. It mentions very concrete cultural entities, and it does so in the context of describing the "end time" in which God will bring sinful history to a close and will usher in the glorious "day of the Lord."

I am aware of the fact that professional biblical scholars—in whose company I do not include myself—make important distinctions when dealing with the Bible's writings about the future, and one such distinction is made between "prophetic" and "apocalyptic" literature. I am also aware of the fact that scholars view the books of Isaiah and Revelation as exemplifying different *kinds* of literature in important respects. I do not deny the importance of introducing such distinctions, but I have chosen to ignore them in the discussion which follows. Whatever the differences in literary mode, Isaiah and Revelation do exhibit some common themes, especially in their focus on a future city which the Lord has prepared for his people. Indeed, it seems obvious that the writer of the Book of Revelation was very conscious of chapter 60 of Isaiah. We do not need to ignore those connecting lines which the biblical writers themselves have drawn.

Isaiah 60 records a vision of a magnificent city. In it the prophet is speaking *to* the city, calling attention to various aspects of its appearance. His tone is joyful, his mood excited. This city is not like any other that he has seen among the products of human efforts at urbanization; it is a city built by God.

Sometimes Isaiah addresses the city in the present tense; at other points he employs the language of future fulfillment. Though the city has not yet been established, he is certain that it will someday arrive. It is clearly a transformed city. Many of the people and objects from Isaiah's own day appear within its walls, but they have assumed different roles, they perform new functions.

Scholars disagree about when this chapter was written. Some believe that it comes from a period before the Hebrew people were forced into exile. Others think it was written during the time of exile. Still others think it was penned during the time just after some of God's people, scattered by the dispersion, began to return to Jerusalem.

For our purposes here, we do not have to resolve this dispute. It is clear that Isaiah was anticipating a day when Jerusalem would be a very different city from the one which he presently encountered. It does not matter whether he envisioned this development out of a prophetic empathy for the alienation that would be experienced in a future exile, or whether his hope was shaped by an actual experience of separation from the homeland. In either case, he is looking forward with the eyes of faith to a time of transformation.

Scholars also disagree about the authorship of the Book of Isaiah. Very conservative scholars have insisted on a single author. Others have argued that the book is a compilation of the writings of two or more authors, writing in different historical periods. Here too we need not attempt to take sides in such debates. Throughout this discussion I will refer to ''Isaiah'' as the author of the entire book. (Similarly, I will refer to the author of Revelation as ''John,'' even though the question of authorship is disputed.) Those who have strong convictions on the critical questions involved may translate my usage into the terms of their own theories.

I will presuppose, however, that the Book of Isaiah is a *unified* work with regard to its message. For example, in what follows I will compare Isaiah 2 with Isaiah 60. In the former chapter the writer speaks very negatively about items which are treated quite positively in the latter chapter. But there is no need to entertain thoughts of ''contradictions'' in order to account for these differing emphases; indeed, the fact that in each of these chapters the writer is struggling with the question of God's attitude toward a common set of entities—for example, the ships of Tarshish and the lumber of Lebanon—points to a set of concerns which is common to earlier and later portions of the Book of Isaiah.

God's Word is a unity—although the unity is often more like that of a symphony than of a geometry textbook. In this sense, the Book of Isaiah in particular is also a unity. The marvelous vision of chapter 60 draws together images and themes which make their appearance already in the opening chapters of the Book.

The city which Isaiah envisions in chapter 60 is a "magnetic" place—it has drawing power. People and things are flocking to this urban center: they are being "turned" to this city, "gathered" from many places, coming "from afar." That the city has this magnetism is important. Many of the people and things which appear in its midst are not, on some accountings, likely candidates for inclusion within its walls.

This recorded vision is an instance of "predictive prophecy." It is sometimes said that the biblical prophets issued two kinds of messages: "forth-telling" and "fore-telling." This chapter is surely an instance of the latter. Isaiah is not merely engaging in utopian speculation or idle daydreaming; he is looking into the future under the guidance of God's Spirit. He is being given a glimpse of things which the Lord will surely bring to pass: "I am the Lord; in its time I will hasten it" (v. 22).* Isaiah's vision, then, is God-given, a revelation in which God tells his people what will happen in the future.

It is also true, of course, that this is *Isaiah's* vision. It is given to *him*, a unique individual, and undoubtedly differs in important ways from one that God might give to Jeremiah or Paul or Priscilla. The Lord gave Isaiah this vision, this "fore-telling," to aid him in his "forth-telling" to his own people. Thus this vision was given to a specific person for a specific people at a specific time in history. It was addressed to particular hopes and fears which were in turn shaped by unique cultural experiences.

But it is also a vision that is given to the people of God in every age, including our own. The hope for a prospering city, a permanent dwelling-place for God's redeemed people, is expressed regularly in the Old Testament. The writer of the Epistle to the Hebrews summarizes the careers of a long list of Old Testament figures by observing that they were all "seeking a homeland"—a quest that will be honored by the God who "has prepared for them a city" (Heb. 11:14, 16). This quest

*Unless otherwise noted, all biblical quotations are from the RSV.

is a New Testament hope as well; in the final chapters of the Bible the writer of the Book of Revelation is also given a vision of a transformed city which is yet to appear—a vision which, as we have already suggested, has important similarities to Isaiah's.

When did Isaiah think that this hope for a transformed city would be fulfilled? How, in his mind, would God establish such a city? It is difficult for us to answer these questions. Perhaps Isaiah thought that the fulfillment was coming very soon—perhaps he even thought that the process of fulfillment had already been set in motion. But he did not see the complete fulfillment in his own lifetime, nor has it occurred yet. No city which has ever appeared in history even closely approximates the description that we are given in Isaiah 60.

There is a sense in which Isaiah understood his vision better than we can today. But there is another sense, an important one, in which we can view his vision from a more privileged position than his vantage point. We have the lessons of further history at our disposal. More importantly, we have been given the fuller revelation, which has been made possible by the apostolic witness to the coming of Jesus Christ.

Like the Old Testament saints, we Christians await the appearance of God's city. We too "desire a better country, that is, a heavenly one" (Heb. 11:16). But while we are to be a "waiting" people, we are not to be passive in our lives of anticipation. The biblical visions of the future are given to us so that we may have the kind of hope that issues forth into lives of active disobedience in the context of contemporary culture.

When I refer to "culture" in these pages I am not using the term in any narrow sense. This is not a book, for example, about "refined tastes" in art or music or literature. My focus here is on the broad patterns of social life, including political, economic, technological, artistic, familial, and educational patterns. It is my contention in these meditations that it is extremely significant that when Isaiah looks to the fulfillment of God's promises, he envisions a community into which technological artifacts, political rulers, and people from many nations are gathered. God intended from the beginning that human beings would "fill the earth" with the processes, patterns, and products of cultural formation. And this intention has in no way been canceled by human sin. God will redeem and transform that which is presently perverted and distorted by human disobedience to his will.

I do not think that I will be able to "prove" this contention in any strict sense. It is quite possible, for example, that someone might want to resist my line of argument by insisting that the passages which I discuss ought not to be submitted to the kind of detailed examination which I give here. Instead—it could be argued—they must be treated "typologically" or as "doxological hyperbole." Even though it may be possible to sustain a perspective of that sort, my own approach has, I think, the advantage of providing us with a plausible reading of the actual details of the passages in question—a reading which, it seems to me, illuminates many other elements in the biblical story.

Isaiah 60

Arise, shine; for your light has come,
    and the glory of the Lord has risen upon you.
For behold, darkness shall cover the earth,
    and thick darkness the peoples;
but the Lord will arise upon you,
    and his glory will be seen upon you.
And nations shall come to your light,
    and kings to the brightness of your risings.

Lift up your eyes round about, and see;
    they all gather together, they come to you;
your sons shall come from far,
    and your daughters shall be carried in the arms.
Then you shall see and be radiant,
    your heart shall thrill and rejoice;
because the abundance of the sea shall be turned to you,
    the wealth of the nations shall come to you.
A multitude of camels shall cover you,
    the young camels of Midian and Ephah;
    all those from Sheba shall come.
They shall bring gold and frankincense,
    and shall proclaim the praise of the Lord.
All the flocks of Kedar shall be gathered to you,
    the rams of Nebaioth shall minister to you;
they shall come up with acceptance on my altar,
    and I will glorify my glorious house.

Who are these that fly like a cloud,
    and like doves to their windows?

1

For the coastlands shall wait for me,
  the ships of Tarshish first,
to bring your sons from far,
  their silver and gold with them,
for the name of the Lord your God,
  and for the Holy One of Israel,
  because he has glorified you.

Foreigners shall build up your walls,
  and their kings shall minister to you;
for in my wrath I smote you,
  but in my favor I have had mercy on you.
Your gates shall be open continually;
  day and night they shall not be shut;
that men may bring to you the wealth of the nations,
  with their kings led in procession.
For the nation and kingdom
  that will not serve you shall perish;
  those nations shall be utterly laid waste.
The glory of Lebanon shall come to you,
  the cypress, the plane, and the pine,
to beautify the place of my sanctuary;
  and I will make the place of my feet glorious.
The sons of those who oppressed you
  shall come bending low to you;
and all who despised you
  shall bow down at your feet;
they shall call you the City of the Lord,
  the Zion of the Holy One of Israel.

Whereas you have been forsaken and hated,
  with no one passing through,
I will make you majestic for ever,
  a joy from age to age.
You shall suck the milk of nations,
  you shall suck the breast of kings;
and you shall know that I, the Lord, am your Saviour
  and your Redeemer, the Mighty One of Jacob.

Instead of bronze I will bring gold,
  and instead of iron I will bring silver;
instead of wood, bronze,
  instead of stones, iron.
I will make your overseers peace,
  and your taskmasters righteousness.
Violence shall no more be heard in your land,
  devastation or destruction within your borders;
you shall call your walls Salvation,
  and your gates Praise.

The sun shall be no more
  your light by day,
nor for brightness shall the moon
  give light to you by night;
but the Lord will be your everlasting light,
  and your God will be your glory.
Your sun shall no more go down,
  nor your moon withdraw itself;
for the Lord will be your everlasting light,
  and your days of mourning shall be ended.
Your people shall all be righteous;
  they shall possess the land for ever,
the shoot of my planting, the work of my hands,
  that I might be glorified.
The least one shall become a clan,
  and the smallest one a mighty nation;
I am the Lord;
  in its time I will hasten it.

What Are the Ships of Tarshish Doing Here?

Describing the Holy City is one way in which the biblical writers portray what we commonly refer to as "heaven" or "the afterlife." My own impression is that we are meant to make this portrayal central to our understanding of the heavenly condition. And, indeed, Christians of various persuasions have made the imagery of the Holy City prominent in their pieties. During my own spiritual upbringing I was exposed to the hymns and songs of several varieties of Protestantism. In the Dutch Calvinist "Christian school" which I attended for several years, we regularly sang about the "City four-square" that stood in "the land of fadeless day." In fundamentalist youth groups I was taught to express the conviction that "I've got a mansion just over the hilltop, in that fair land where we'll never grow old." And at more "ecumenical" gatherings I heard Christians pray:

> Give us, O God, the strength to build
> The City that hath stood
> Too long a dream, whose laws are love,
> Whose ways are brotherhood.

In my childhood, then, imagery of the Holy City figured prominently in our language about the future. But if you were to have asked me during those times to describe what heaven would be like—"really" like—I suspect that I would not have used this imagery in my response. I would have been much more inclined to talk about a "spiritual" realm to which a bodiless soul goes in order to be with God. And I suspect that what was true of me then is still the case for many Christians today.

5

There is, I think, a plausible explanation for this kind of "de-mythologizing." In the New Testament scheme there are at least two stages of the afterlife which must be taken into account. One is the condition of those believers who have died before the end of history. Where, we might ask, is Catherine Booth now? The Bible doesn't give a very detailed account of her present condition. But it does assure us that when Christians are "away from the body" they are "at home with the Lord" (II Cor. 5:8), because death cannot separate a believer from the love of God (Rom. 8:38-39).

But this condition is only an "interim" or an "intermediate state" in which believers who have died are waiting for something further to happen. It is, in short, a condition of "waiting for the Resurrection." Christians' bodiless presence with the Lord is not the final state of blessedness. Our ultimate goal is to be raised up for new life, a resurrected life in which we will realize our true destinies as followers of Jesus Christ. And it is with regard to this condition, our ultimate goal, that the biblical imagery of the Holy City must be viewed as central.

The Christian life is directed toward a City, a place in which God's redemptive purposes for his creation will be realized. If we think of the future life as a disembodied existence in an ethereal realm—which is not, I have suggested, our ultimate goal—then it is difficult to think of our present cultural affairs as in any sense a positive preparation for heavenly existence. But if we think of the future life in terms of inhabiting a Heavenly City, we have grounds for looking for some patterns of continuity between our present lives and the life to come. The Bible, I think, encourages us to think in these terms.

Nothing that is said in these meditations should be taken as suggesting that we can in any significant way "build" the Holy City here and now. The Holy City comes "down out of heaven from God" (Rev. 21:2); the Lord is its "builder and maker" (Heb. 11:10). The arrival of this City will constitute a radical break with the present patterns of sinful life.

But the Holy City is not *wholly* discontinuous with present conditions. The biblical glimpses of this City give us reason to think that its contents will not be completely unfamiliar to people like us. In fact, the contents of the City will be more akin to our present cultural patterns than is usually acknowledged in discussions of the afterlife.

Isaiah pictures the Holy City as a center of commerce, a place which receives the vessels, goods, and currency of commercial activity. Camels come from Midian, Ephah, and Sheba, carrying gold and frankincense (v. 6). The City receives the flocks of Kedar and the rams of Nebaioth (v. 7). Ships from Tarshish, bearing silver and gold, sail into the City's harbor (v. 9). And costly lumber—the cypress, the plane, and the pine—is imported from Lebanon (v. 13). Animal, vegetable, mineral—they are all brought into the renewed Jerusalem.

When I was a boy I asked my mother whether God would allow my pet dog to go to heaven when he died. Several years ago my own son asked me the same question about his dog. As I remember the two exchanges, I answered my son's question in a manner similar to the way my mother answered mine: "Well, dogs don't have souls, you see. But anything is possible with God. He will do what is best for us."

I still don't have strong views about whether either of those two particular dogs will be resurrected. But I do worry about the assumptions of the argument that I recited in answer to the question. Why do we assume that only things with "souls" will participate in the New Age? Isaiah certainly is not committed to that assumption. He has no problem with the idea that the Holy City will be populated by many animals.

There are several points at which Isaiah mentions animals in the context of describing God's future work of redemption. In a well-known passage in chapter 11, for example, Isaiah describes how animals will act toward each other and toward humans in that day when "the earth shall be full of the knowledge of the Lord":

> The wolf shall dwell with the lamb,
> and the leopard shall lie down with the kid,
> and the calf and the lion and the fatling together,
> and a little child shall lead them.
> The cow and the bear shall feed;
> their young shall lie down together;

and the lion shall eat straw like the ox.
The sucking child shall play over the hole of the asp,
and the weaned child shall put his hand on the
    adder's den. (vv. 6-8)

In the glorious future the Lord will eliminate conflict between animals, and between animals and human beings. Former predators will live peacefully with their former prey. Little children will have nothing to fear from beasts or snakes.

The coming of the peace, the *shalom*, of the Lord has far-reaching implications. The fullness of the knowledge of the Lord will banish all hostility and enmity from the good creation. The curse of sin will be lifted from the earth, and God's righteousness will heal all that was touched by it. Even relationships among the animals will be transformed. This is Isaiah's meaning in the passage in chapter 11.

But this is not the point of the animals' appearance in the transformed City described in chapter 60. Here the animals mentioned are primarily important as commercial goods and vehicles. Sheep and rams are items to be bought and sold; camels are beasts of burden, the ''ships of the desert.'' Ancient nations who possessed them had economic power and mobility, and physical signs of wealth and prestige. The nations who possessed them in great numbers were to be admired and respected.

And now these animals, along with sailing ships and lumber and precious metals, appear in the transformed City. This thought must have been a pleasant surprise for Isaiah and his hearers. They had undoubtedly been awed when they witnessed the displays of technological, cultural, military, and commercial power of other nations. It is likely that they envied Ephah's camels and Nebaioth's rams and Lebanon's lumber, signs of the commercial and political power of these neighboring nations.

And now these entities are gathered into the renewed Jerusalem. But as they appear in this transformed commercial center, they are no longer signs of *pagan* cultural strength or displays of alien power. Nor are they objects to be envied from a distance. Here in the transformed City these vessels and goods serve a very different purpose.

Isaiah is very explicit about this new purpose, noting what function each creature and item now performs. Ephah's camels now "proclaim the praise of the Lord" (v. 6). Nebaioth's rams "shall minister to you" as acceptable sacrifices on the Lord's altars (v. 7). The ships of Tarshish bring precious metals "for the name of the Lord your God" (v. 9). And the costly lumber from Lebanon will "beautify the place of my sanctuary" (v. 13). Each of the items mentioned is now to be put to the service of God and his people.

None of this is very helpful in deciding whether your cat or my dog will be in heaven. But it is instructive to see just *why* Isaiah's inclusion of animals and other non-human entities in the Holy City has little to do with our eschatological concerns about our own pets. When *we* wonder about heaven we often limit our attention to questions about how much of "me" or "mine" will be carried over into eternity. Will I still be able to pet Rover? Will Irving still be "my husband"? Will I be able to play golf or collect stamps? Will I eat in heaven?

But Isaiah seems to be much more interested in "them" and "theirs." When the Day of the Lord arrives, what will become of the sailing fleet of Tarshish? Is there any future in Kedar's sheep-raising business? How will all of the silver and gold in the world finally be disposed of?

Isaiah's interests are more "cosmic" than ours often appear to be. Isaiah is, in contemporary jargon, interested in the future of "corporate structures" and "cultural patterns." And his vision leads him to what are for many of us very surprising observations about the future destiny of many items of "pagan culture." He sees these items as being gathered into the Holy City to be put to good use there. Thus, not only are his questions different from the ones we often ask about the afterlife, but his answers are different from those which many of us might give. If we were to ask Isaiah's questions (about the future destiny of the items he mentions) in most contemporary gatherings of Christians, we would probably get much more negative answers. We—at least many of us—seem to assume that the present patterns and entities of corporate life will simply be done away with when the time for "heaven" comes.

Why is that? Why would the idea that pagan items will appear in the Heavenly City be such a strange one to many contemporary Christians? Why do many Christians today ignore the prophetic announcement that "the wealth of the nations" (Isa. 60:5) and "the glory and the honor of the nations" (Rev. 21:26) will be brought into the Holy City?

The problem is, I think, that it is so difficult to square this theme—at first glance, at least—with other things which we read about in the Scriptures. Doesn't the Bible teach that the Lord will someday destroy the wicked and their works? Aren't there many places in the Scriptures where we read that God will judge the patterns and products of pagan culture?

We do indeed find these very negative assessments of pagan culture in the Bible. There can be no denying that the biblical writers speak many times of God's judgment on all of the doers and works of unrighteousness. God's wrath will be poured out, in seemingly destructive ways, on the agents and patterns and products of pagan culture.

The puzzle here is made even more complicated by the fact that the very writers who describe the Holy City as receiving the works of pagan cultures are the same ones who speak so strongly of God's wrathful judgment on those cultures. John, who envisions "the glory and the honor of the nations" being brought into the Holy City, has described in an earlier chapter the destruction of the glory of the wicked city of Babylon: the merchants who had profited from Babylon's wealth cry out in anguish, " 'In one hour all this wealth has been laid waste' " (Rev. 18:15-17).

Isaiah's passages describing God's judgment are even more difficult to understand, since he seems to picture God as destroying the same kinds of things which are then brought into the Holy City in chapter 60. In chapter 2 Isaiah speaks of a time of judgment that is coming against the prideful patterns of rebellious nations. God's people, he complains, have chosen to imitate the lives of their sinful neighbors. They have envied those pagan nations who possess precious metals and many horses and chariots, and who "bow down to the work of their hands, to what their own fingers have made" (vv. 7-8). What God's people fail to realize is that these nations who take great pride in their own technological and military strength are thereby *idolatrous* nations. They will someday be brought low by the power of God, for "the Lord alone will be exalted in that day" (v. 11).

At this point in his message in chapter 2, Isaiah goes on to list the actual items which are the sources of pagan pride, pronouncing the coming judgment of God on these instruments of rebellion. In the light of the vision described in chapter 60, the list here is a very interesting one:

> For the Lord of hosts has a day
> against all that is proud and lofty,
> against all that is lifted up and high;
> against all the cedars of Lebanon, lofty and lifted
>   up;
> and against all the oaks of Bashan;
> against all the high mountains,
> and against all the lofty hills;
> against every high tower,
> and against every fortified wall;
> against all the ships of Tarshish,
> and against all the beautiful craft.
> And the haughtiness of man shall be humbled,
> and the pride of men shall be brought low;
> and the Lord alone shall be exalted in that day.
>
> (vv. 12-17)

We find in this list many of the same kinds of things—indeed, in a few instances, the very same items—whose presence we have noted in the transformed City of chapter 60: costly lumber from Lebanon, commercial vessels and other "beautiful crafts." The means of military protection—hills, mountains, and towers—are also explicitly mentioned.

All of these things will be judged by the Lord, according to chapter 2, because they are "proud and lofty." People trust in these things for their security; nations point to these possessions as signs of their corporate strength. But a day is coming, Isaiah says, when all of these things will be "brought low," rendered useless as grounds for prideful boastings. Only the Lord will be exalted on that final day of accounting.

Thus our puzzle. How can the very things which, according to Isaiah 2, will experience God's wrath appear, in Isaiah 60, as instruments of service to God and God's people? The ships of Tarshish are an interesting case in point here, since they are mentioned explicitly in both places.

Scholars have not been able to ascertain exactly what is meant by the Old Testament references to "Tarshish." It may have been a place which Isaiah and his contemporaries knew quite a bit about. Or it may not have referred to a specific place at all, but may have functioned as a shorthand for something like "the farther regions." Or it may have been a very distant region about which they actually knew very little, but about which they had formed an idealized conception.

It would be nice to know what "Tarshish" refers to, but it really isn't necessary for our present purposes. The scholars do seem to agree that the "ships of Tarshish" were very large vessels, capable of carrying heavy loads for long distances. And there can be no doubt that Isaiah and his contemporaries considered these ships to be very impressive vessels. They were possessions which engendered pride in their owners and crews, instruments of pagan commercial power. Therefore in Isaiah 2 these "beautiful craft" are mentioned as examples of entities which are "proud and lofty . . . lifted up and high." And because of this, "the Lord of hosts has a day . . . against all the ships of Tarshish," a theme which is repeated in Psalm 48, where we read that the Lord will "shatter the ships of Tarshish" (v. 7).

How are we to understand this negative message in relation to the more positive one that we have noted? If the ships of Tarshish are to be destroyed because of their wickedness, how can they turn up in the Holy City as instruments of service to the Lord?

One way out of the dilemma, of course, is to decide that Isaiah is confused, even to the point of contradicting himself. If we take this view we simply have two very different accounts within the Bible, and, more specifically, within the book of Isaiah, explaining how God will finally deal with the "stuff" of pagan culture. According to one account, God will finally destroy such things as the ships of Tarshish; according to the other, God will in some sense redeem them in the end time. Since these are conflicting accounts, anyone who wants a consistent, biblically grounded view will simply have to make a choice. Or live with the contradiction—perhaps by labeling it a "mystery."

But there are many reasons why we ought not to settle for such a view. One good reason is that a more plausible understanding of the situation is available. There is no need to read the negative passages as insisting that these pagan entities *as such* will be destroyed. Indeed, we would do well to be cautious in our interpretations whenever we read in the Bible about God's destructive judgments. Sometimes the writers are describing what *could* happen to wicked people if they were to get what they deserved. At other times images are used, such as fire, in such a way that they are referring to a purifying divine judgment, not an annihilating one.

My own impression is that the judgment that will visit the ships of Tarshish is of a purifying sort. We might think here of the "breaking" of the ships of Tarshish as more like the breaking of a horse rather than the breaking of a vase. The judgment here is meant to *tame,* not destroy. The ships of Tarshish will be harnessed for service in the Holy City—a process which will require a "breaking" of sorts.

It is not, then, the ships *as such* that will be destroyed; it is their former *function* that will perish. It is worth noting that it was a ship from Tarshish which Jonah boarded to flee from the call of the Lord (Jonah 1:3). This incident aptly suggests the ships' pagan function, because they are means of rebellion against God. They are vessels used to flee from his presence, instruments designed to thwart his will.

God's judgment is meant to destroy this paganness. "Wail, O ships of Tarshish, for your stronghold is laid waste" (Isa. 23:14). When these ships are thus stripped of the haughtiness and rebellion with which they are presently associated, they are freed for service to the Lord and his people. They become vessels for ministry in the transformed City.

A similar pattern applies to the trees that grow in Lebanon. The Lord "will cut down the thickets of the forest with an axe, and Lebanon with its majestic trees will fall" (Isa. 10:34). This could, of course, be an image of destruction. But it could also be meant to picture the way that the Lord will re-shape Lebanon's lumber. And that seems to be the proper interpretation, given the message of Isaiah 60—that wood from Lebanon will be used in the Holy City to beautify the Lord's sanctuary (v. 13).

What is the relationship between "fore-telling" and "forth-telling" here? In what way, if any, was this information about the future meant to influence how Isaiah's hearers were to live in the present? Well, it seems clear that while Isaiah is in some sense optimistic about the future of many elements of pagan culture, this was not meant to encourage God's people to embrace that culture in its present forms. Simply to "affirm" the ships of Tarshish and the cedars of Lebanon as they presently exist would be to miss that half of Isaiah's message that expresses judgment. And nothing in Isaiah's account of the future City is meant to detract from an emphasis on God's rejection of pagan culture in its present form.

God's people are not to covet the possessions of pagan neighbors. They must not envy the material wealth, the precious metals, the horses and chariots, the vessels of trade and war, the military fortifications that their neighbors boast about. To covet such items would be to show an insensitivity to the idolatrous functions of those instruments in their pagan cultural contexts. In purely human terms, of course, the house of Jacob has a right to be awed by displays of commercial, technological, and military power. But succumbing to this awe would be failing to remember their own identity as a nation that is reliant upon God alone. As Zechariah put it, "Not by might, nor by power, but by my Spirit, says the Lord of hosts" (Zech. 4:6).

And so, whenever God's people are tempted to look for security from a source other than God's protecting Spirit—or whenever they are inclined to "supplement" the power of God with military or technological means—they are condemned by the prophets. Only God must be exalted as the defender of his people. No other force—whether it appears in the shape of wealth or chariots or sailing vessels or strong fortifications—can successfully thwart his will. All such things will be "brought low" by the mighty hand of the Lord.

But, as has been suggested, the "bringing low" here does not mean destruction but transformation. It is not the camels or the ships or the gold or the lumber which will be destroyed in the final conflict. Rather, it is the rebellious *uses*, the idolatrous *functions*, which seem under present conditions to be inextricably intertwined with these artifacts.

Thus, God's people must wait until the Lord brings his redemptive purposes to fruition. The house of Jacob will receive the things which they presently envy—but only after those instruments have been transformed into fitting vessels of service, cleansed of their idolatrous functions. There must be a healing of "the wealth of the nations."

God's present attitude, then, toward these instruments of culture is an ambivalent one. As tools of human rebellion and objects of idolatrous trust, he hates them—and he warns his people not to be contaminated by them. But he hates them because of their present uses. And his hatred will lead him to transform them into proper instruments of service.

God's people must imitate God's attitude. They too must hate those things which cause their idolatrous neighbors to boast. But their hatred must take the form of waiting for the day of transformation, when the camels of Ephah and the ships of Tarshish will be made into fitting vessels of service for the Lord and his people.

It is worth pointing out that the Apostle Paul struggles with the question of eating meat that has been offered to idols in a manner that almost parallels our discussion of the judgment-transformation pattern in Isaiah. In I Corinthians 8 he argues that food that has been offered to idols cannot harm the Christian if that person has the proper "knowledge" of the situation: "we know that 'an idol has no real existence,' and that 'there is no God but one' " (v. 4)—therefore "we are no worse off if we do not eat, and no better off if we do" (v. 8). Christians are free to partake or to refrain, a liberty limited only by a concern for those who are not mature in the faith.

Later in chapter 10, Paul advises Christians to "shun the worship of idols" (v. 14). Having done that, he says they can "eat whatever is sold in the meat market without raising any question on the ground of conscience" (v. 25). His basis for recognizing the Christian's liberty in this area is an appeal to God's creating activity (here he quotes the Psalmist): "the earth is the Lord's, and everything in it" (v. 26).

In addressing this very specific practice Paul makes an emphasis that is similar to Isaiah's. The goods and artifacts used in idolatrous ways are, nonetheless, things made by God's hand. Pagan nations are misusing what is in fact God's good creation. God will punish them for the ways in which they have perverted and distorted the things which he has provided, but he never loses sight of his good creation. He must reclaim that which humans have used to rebel against him.

In the end time, God will "make all things new" (Rev. 21:5). In order to renew and transform his good creation, he must purge it of all rebellion and idolatry: "as for the cowardly, the faithless, the polluted, as for murderers, fornicators, sorcerers, idolaters, and all liars, their lot shall be in the lake that burns with fire and sulphur, which is the second death" (Rev. 21:8). But God will not destroy the things which they have put to their own rebellious uses. The new Jerusalem will be bedecked with jewels and metals gathered from the nations of the earth; and "the glory and the honor of the nations" will be brought into the transformed City (Rev. 21:26).

But why is God so interested in gathering in this "glory" and "honor" and "wealth" from the nations? It is helpful to keep in mind Paul's citation of the Psalmist: "The earth is the Lord's, and everything in it." The actual wording in Psalm 24:1 is even a little more helpful for our present purposes: "The earth is the Lord's and the fulness thereof."

The "fulness," or the "filling," of the earth belongs to God. When God created all things in the beginning, he appointed the first man and woman to be stewards over the earth's resources. He told them to " 'fill the earth and subdue it' " (Gen. 1:28). The command to "fill" the earth here is not merely a divine request that Adam and Eve have a lot of babies. The earth was also to be "filled" by the broader patterns of their interactions with nature and with each other. They would bring order to the Garden. They would introduce schemes for managing its affairs. To "subdue" the Garden would be to transform untamed nature into a social environment. In these ways human beings would be "adding" to that which God created. This is the kind of "filling" that some Christians have had in mind when they have labeled this command in Genesis 1—helpfully, I think—"the cultural mandate." God placed human beings in his creation in order to introduce a cultural "filling" in ways that conformed to his divine will.

But human beings rebelled against God. This meant, among other things, that they violated God's mandate to form culture out of a faithful obedience to his will. The history of human cultural formation, then, is one of perverting the good creation; men and women have "filled" and "subdued" the earth in faithless ways—in their family lives, their art, their political dealings, their economic patterns, their technology, their educational endeavors. In these areas and in others as well, human beings have distorted the process of "filling" and "subduing" that was originally intended to develop along obedient and faithful lines.

But God has not abandoned his good creation, even in its presently distorted form. The earth's "filling" still belongs to him. He sent his own Son to rescue the entire cosmos from the effects of sin, and his rescue efforts take into account the facts of sinful historical development. As a number of writers have noted, the Bible begins with a Garden and ends with a City. When God originally created, he formed a rural place for human beings to occupy. But in bringing in his new creation, he will not recreate the original Garden. In the end time, the product of God's transforming work will be a renewed City.

There is an important sense in which the Holy City is the Garden-plus-the-"filling." During the course of history sinful human beings have created a perverse "filling." The things which they have added to the Garden are, contrary to the Creator's intentions, perverse and idolatrous. But God still insists that the "filling" belongs to him. And he will reclaim it at the end time, in doing so transforming it into the kind of "filling" that he originally intended for his creation. This is why the "wealth" and the "glory" and the "honor" of the nations must be gathered in when the Day of the Lord arrives. God's ownership over the "filling" must be vindicated at the end of history.

Human beings have continued to fill the earth since Isaiah's day. And the earth and all that is in it still belongs to God. Therefore it takes little imagination to see that Isaiah's message must somehow apply to our own day. We must not envy those instruments of commercial, technological, and military strength which cause people to boast today. God alone is our protector. Only the Lord is worthy of our ultimate obedience and trust. Recognizing that God still intends to renew his creation, we must wait confidently for the appearance of the transformed City, when the ships of Tarshish will sail into the harbor, bearing silver and gold to the glory of God.

But we cannot be content to confine our attention to the same entities which Isaiah envisioned. God will gather in the ships of Tarshish, we have said, because he takes history seriously. But much has occurred in history since Isaiah's day, and God takes this further history seriously as well. So, as we think about what will be gathered into the Holy City, we must look for present-day analogues to the ships of Tarshish and the cedars of Lebanon.

What are the "proud and lofty" things of contemporary cultures? To what do nations and peoples point in showing off their "honor" and "glory"? It would be interesting to count how many times those very words—"honor" and "glory" and their variants and equivalents—are used at, say, patriotic rallys. The variants are seemingly endless. "National honor." "Our honor is at stake." "We are gathered today to honor those who. . . ." "Our glorious heritage." "Our glorious flag." "What a glorious nation we live in!"

People boast about the nations of which they are citizens. They also boast about ethnic identities, religious affiliations, race, gender, and clan. They point in pride to natural wonders which they claim as their own possessions—"This land was made for you and me." They show off their military might, their economic clout, their material abundance.

The Lord of hosts has a day against all of these things: against nations who brag about being "Number One," against racist pride, against the idealizing of "human potential," against the manifestos of the "me generation," against missiles and bombs, against art and technology, against philosophy textbooks and country music records, against Russian vodka and South African diamonds, against trade centers and computer banks, against throne-rooms and presidential memorabilia. In short, God will stand in judgment of all idolatrous and prideful attachments to military, technological, commercial, and cultural might. He will destroy all of those rebellious projects which glorify oppression, exploitation, and the accumulation of possessions. It is in such projects that we can discern today our own ships of Tarshish and cedars from Lebanon.

But the "stuff" of human cultural rebellion will nonetheless be gathered into the Holy City. God still owns the "filling." The earth—including the American military and French art and Chinese medicine and Nigerian agriculture—belongs to the Lord. And he will reclaim all of these things, harnessing them for service in the City.

But, you may ask, isn't this stretching the point a bit? Will *all* of the works of culture be gathered into the Holy City? What about intercontinental missiles or nuclear submarines? Or pornographic movies? Or posters which exhibit Lenin's face? Or the Mafia's accounting books?

Isaiah seems to be sensitive to these kinds of questions. The things which he mentions in chapter 60—those pagan entities which will be put to good use in the Holy City—are items which seem quite capable of being employed in a "redeemed" environment. But it is important to note that there are, for example, no military armaments mentioned in chapter 60. It is not clear what God's people would *do* with swords and spears in the City where peace and righteousness are the rule of the day.

It might be interesting, of course, to have a museum for such artifacts in the Holy City. It might be very instructive for us, when we become citizens of the New Jerusalem, to gaze upon those perverse instruments of human corruption which figured so prominently in the sinful order of things. But Isaiah does not mention this possibility. Instead, he depicts—early on in his book—the weapons of war as being transformed into instruments which *can* be put to good use in the transformed commonwealth: the Lord will "beat their swords into plowshares, and their spears into pruning hooks" (Isa. 2:4).

Not all of the items of pagan culture will be gathered, as is, into the Holy City. A pagan ship will be changed into a redeemed ship—but it will still be a ship. But other things will have to have their identities, their basic functions, transformed; some of them will be changed almost beyond recognition. Swords will become plowshares. Spears will be changed into pruning hooks. Marxist posters will become aesthetic objects which will enhance the beauty of the City. Perhaps missiles will become play areas for children.

Once again, the emphasis here is on transformation, not destruction. God is still pictured as working *with* the "filling."

Needless to say, there is much that remains mysterious here. But the element of mystery also pervades the more "personal" dimension of belief in the afterlife. As individuals we look forward to the day when we will be transformed, but it is difficult for us to imagine what that will be like: "Beloved, we are God's children now; it does not yet appear what we shall be" (I John 3:2). We will not be completely annihilated, replaced by some totally different persons, but each of us will be transformed.

It is difficult, then, for us to know what we will be like as heavenly beings. But we do know that God will work, in each of our cases, with what he originally created. *We* will be transformed. God will re-create *us*. A thread of personal identity reaches from the "now" to the "shall be."

What applies on this level of personal destiny seems to hold true for the whole creation, including its cultural dimensions. God will work with what he has created and with the "filling" which human beings have added to what he made in the beginning. The fruits of history—even sinful history—will be gathered into the City, and made into fitting vessels of service.

"So, whether you eat or drink, or whatever you do, do all to the glory of God" (I Cor. 10:31). We do not have to abandon the works of human culture to the Devil. All of the commercial and technological and military "stuff" that we see around us still belongs to the world which God has made and will someday redeem. Simply knowing that this is the case, of course, does not generate easy answers to many difficult practical questions (some of which we will address later).

But we must first of all allow this knowledge to shape the basic attitudes and expectations that we bring to our wrestling with the practical questions. We must train ourselves to look at the worlds of commerce and art and recreation and education and technology, and confess that all of this "filling" belongs to God. And then we must engage in the difficult business of finding patterns of cultural involvement which are consistent with that confession. If, in a fundamental and profound sense, God has not given up on human culture, then neither must we.

''The earth is the Lord's, and everything in it''—even the ships of Tarshish.

When the Kings Come Marching In

Belief in an afterlife has figured prominently in both attacks upon and defenses of the Christian faith. Critics of Christianity have regularly dragged out the "pie in the sky" argument. Belief in heaven, they argue, serves as an excuse for Christian inaction. All sorts of evils and inequities can be tolerated by people who believe that this world will someday give way to a blissful paradise. Belief in heaven, then, serves as a means for reinforcing the status quo.

Defenders of Christianity have, on the other hand, argued that a belief in an afterlife satisfies convictions and longings which are deeply embedded in the human spirit. Like the attackers, these defenders also point to the existence of many evils and inequities in the world. But it is simply a fact, they insist, that many of these wrongs will go uncorrected in this present life—even though Christians are obligated to fight against evil. If the world as we presently know it is all that there is or ever will be, then there will never be retribution for all of the injustices that human beings have experienced in history. But, they go on to argue, the thought that the debts caused by human evil will go unrequited is deeply repugnant. Thus there must be some sort of final accounting. And since this kind of reckoning does not take place in life as we know it now, there must be an afterlife.

When looked at as "proofs," neither of these lines of argument is very satisfactory. But if we employ more relaxed standards, each has some merit. The critics of the Christian belief in an afterlife are certainly correct in criticizing the ways in which this belief has often actually functioned in the hearts and lives of Christian people. "Future hope" *has* often served as a basis for tolerating wickedness in the present age. This is not, contrary to the Marxist argument, the "real" function of Christian belief in an afterlife. But it has in fact functioned that way for many Christians.

But even when a belief in an afterlife is functioning correctly for Christians, it contains an element of "pie in the sky." There is no getting around this fact, and it should not be embarrassing for a Christian to admit it. After all, if the pie is actually in the sky, then a "pie in the sky" belief is very appropriate.

Once again, we must stress the fact that our belief in heaven can give us no good excuse for inaction here and now. We must work diligently for justice and peace and righteousness—the Bible makes that very clear. Our belief in an afterlife cannot replace this kind of diligent activity; rather, it ought to comfort us as we try to do God's will in the present time. For when these efforts are less than completely successful—as they usually are—we can appeal to the biblical promise that complete success will be realized in the New Age.

All of this has a special bearing on the world of politics. Many human ills and wrongs are rooted in political life. Sometimes political systems are directly responsible for evil—as when totalitarian governments deliberately enforce unjust laws and practices. Then there are other evils—such as child abuse and the marketing of unsafe products—which are not directly caused by governments, but which could be avoided or curtailed by more rigorous legislation and law enforcement.

Throughout history, then, many people who have been victimized in one way or another have had a right to accuse governments of acting irresponsibly. And many, perhaps most, of the wrongs for which governments bear direct or indirect responsibility have gone unremedied. Political history has generated a long list of unpaid debts.

If we take seriously the idea that the New Age will be a time for the settling of accounts, we should certainly expect some kind of political transactions to occur in the Holy City. And some Christians *have* viewed the Last Judgment in these terms. When Christian people have experienced political oppression, they have often longed for a day of political vindication. They have viewed God as a righteous judge who will someday set the political record straight. On the other hand,

those Christians who have been relatively satisfied with the
political status quo have tended to think of the afterlife in rather
''a-political'' terms.

Isaiah is on the side of the ''politicizers'' of the afterlife,
a position made clear by the obvious political elements in his
description of the Holy City. Kings will be drawn to the brightness of the City's light (v. 3). Kings from foreign nations will
''minister'' to God's people in the City (v. 10). People from
many nations will lead their rulers ''in procession'' into the
City (v. 11). And God's people will ''suck the breast of kings''
(v. 16).

Who are these political rulers whom Isaiah mentions, and
why are they brought into the Holy City? It is important, I
think, to dispense with the idea that Isaiah is thinking exclusively of ''saved'' rulers. Commentators on these references,
and on the reference to the entrance of ''the kings of the earth''
in Revelation 21:23-25, sometimes try to take refuge in this idea.
They insist that the kings mentioned by Isaiah and John are
political rulers who happen to be believers or who represent
''Christian nations.''

The suggestion that these are ''saved'' kings has been
developed along two different lines. According to one interpretation, these rulers are persons who have accepted, during their lifetimes, God's gracious offer of redemption. We
might think here of specific politicians who have professed faith
in the God of the Bible: King David, Queen Esther, Emperor
Constantine, Queen Wilhelmina, Senator Mark Hatfield. They
are believers who happen to be politicians. By picturing them
as walking the streets of the City, Isaiah and John are celebrat-
ing the fact that there are some ''saved'' political rulers.

A second interpretation treats these references as support
for the idea of ''universal salvation.'' In the biblical scheme,
according to this view, political rulers are associated with the
very dregs of humanity. But in these visions these seemingly
''unsaveable'' types are portrayed as citizens of the Holy City.
Isaiah and John are telling us that even wicked rulers will be
saved in the end. And if these kinds of people will be allowed
into heaven, well, anyone can get in!

If I had to choose between these interpretations, I would

opt for the first one, because it highlights the importance of human decision. It rightly assumes that if political rulers are to enter the Holy City as recipients of the blessings of salvation, it will be because they have responded during their lifetimes to God's offer of salvation. And it also correctly notes that some politicians have made that decision, and that they will be included in the company of the redeemed. The other interpretation, which puts forth the notion that God will someday simply "forgive and forget" the sins of a Nero or a Hitler or a Stalin or an Idi Amin, seems rather silly in contrast.

But neither of these interpretations seems to capture Isaiah's intent here. Both interpretations make the same basic assumption—namely, that if political rulers do enter the Holy City, it is to receive the benefits of eternal salvation. The salvation of individuals is indeed a precious theme in the Scriptures. No biblically grounded vision of the future life can in any way underestimate the importance of the fact that individual sinners have been redeemed by the blood of Christ, and will someday be received into the Heavenly City. Nor may we harbor thoughts of a naive "universalism" in our understanding of the salvation of individuals. The Scriptures call human beings to repentance at the Cross of Jesus. Those who refuse to accept the good news that Jesus is the only true redeemer of humankind must live with the Bible's very real warnings against continuing unbelief. Only the way of the Cross leads home to God's City. In dealing with the biblical message regarding individual destinies, we must honestly face the warning of Scripture: only believers will be saved; the wicked will be cast off.

Why, then, are the kings brought into the City? The answer seems to be that when their entrance into the City is recorded by prophet and apostle, the subject being dealt with is not the salvation of individuals but something else. The final salvation of individuals will take place within the walls of God's City, but there are other transactions which must also occur there.

One of these transactions is the one which we have already discussed: the gathering-in of human cultural "filling." And both Isaiah and John link the entrance of the kings to this transaction. The kings of the earth will bring "the wealth of the nations" into the Holy City.

The power and authority of ancient kings differed in two ways from our understanding of political rule today. It was, we might say, more politically intensive and more non-politically extensive. Within what we think of as the sphere of politics, ancient rulers possessed a very intensive kind of power. Of course, some present-day totalitarian governments almost match ancient governments in this regard. But even where contemporary dictators possess absolute political power, their subjects seldom assume that they *deserve* to exercise that kind of control. In ancient times, however, it was often assumed that political rulers had a right to function as dictators or near-dictators.

But the authority of ancient rulers also extended well beyond the realm of politics. Actually, we can put this point in one of two ways. We can say that the ancient king was more than a political ruler, or we can say that "politics" covered more territory for the ancients than it does for us today.

The ancient office of kingship evolved out of the still more ancient roles of clan leader, tribal chief, leader of the hunt, and the like—and the office absorbed many of these functions. Kings were military leaders (in more than the quasi-ceremonial sense in which the U.S. President is Commander-in-Chief of the Armed Forces) who often led their armies into battle. They were also the chief sponsors of the arts and sciences.

In short, ancient kings served as the primary authorities over the broad patterns of the cultural lives of their nations. And when they stood over against other nations, they were the *bearers*, the *representatives*, of their respective cultures. To assemble kings together, then, was in an important sense to assemble their national cultures together. The king of a given nation could bear, singly, a far-reaching authority that is today divided among many different kinds of leaders: the captains of industry; the molders of public opinion in art, entertainment, and sexuality; educational leaders; representatives of family interests; and so on. This is why Isaiah and John could link the entrance of the kings into the City with the gathering-in of the "wealth of the nations."

Thus ancient kings were more than "political rulers" as we understand the term today—but they were not less than political rulers. They were the heads of government, the rulers over the politics of their respective nations. This too is an important part of their role as they are gathered into the Holy City.

Different notions of political authority operated in the ancient Near East. The Egyptians, for example, viewed their rulers as "divine" beings—a fact that scholarly studies* always introduce by noting that this is a very difficult idea for us moderns to understand. In practical terms, however, this meant that there were very few checks or limits placed on what a pharaoh could decree; his word was taken as having divine authority. The Mesopotamians, on the other hand, viewed their rulers in more "human" terms. Mesopotamian kings were perceived as chosen servants of the gods—although they were not usually understood as "automatic" vehicles for divine revelation. There was an acknowledged gap between the divine will and human rulers.

In each case, however, political rulers were looked to as the primary interpreters of the divine will. But this was not the case in ancient Israel. Indeed, in the earliest stages of Israel's political life there were no human kings at all. God was viewed as the sole King of his people. The task of interpreting the political will of God was given to judges, teachers, and prophets who had a special ability to discern the Lord's will—even, on some occasions, directly conversing with the deity.

But there came a time when the people of Israel wanted to have a human king, "to govern us like all the nations" (I Sam. 8:15). When Samuel transmitted this request to the Lord, God acquiesced with seeming reluctance: " 'Hearken to the voice of the people in all that they say to you; for they have not rejected you, but they have rejected me from being king over them' " (I Sam. 8:7).

*For a good study of this sort, which compares ideas of kingship in the ancient Near East—especially Egypt, Mesopotamia, and Israel—see Henri Frankfort's *Kingship and the Gods: A Study of Ancient Near Eastern Religion as the Integration of Society and Nature* (Chicago: University of Chicago Press, 1948).

Some people think that this episode does not comport well with the prediction regarding it in Deuteronomy 17:14-15:

> "When you come to the land which the Lord your God gives you, and you possess it and dwell in it, and then say, 'I will set a king over me, like all the nations that are round about me'; you may indeed set as king over you him whom the Lord your God will choose. One from among your brethren you shall set as king over you; you may not put a foreigner over you, who is not your brother."

But there is no conflict between the two passages. The above prediction merely sets forth in general terms what will in fact happen, while the episode recounted in I Samuel describes the actual process in more detail. Though God's response to Israel's request is not one of unqualified approval, his disapproval is not directed toward the very idea of having a human king but toward the people's motives for making the request.

When Saul is chosen as Israel's first human king, it becomes clear that this arrangement does not necessarily alter God's covenantal arrangement with his people. For when Samuel, having warned the people of the corruption and manipulation which will result from their choice (I Sam. 8:11-18), does designate Saul as king, he spells out the provisions whereby the new arrangement could be one of divine blessing: "Behold, the Lord has set a king over you. If you will fear the Lord and serve him and hearken to his voice and not rebel against the commandment of the Lord, and if both you and the king who reigns over you will follow the Lord your God, it will be well" (I Sam. 12:13-14).

But it was not always "well" with the human politics of God's people. Sometimes a given king was viewed as a genuine blessing from God, anointed by God to promote righteousness and peace (see Psalm 72). But these experiences were mixed with ones of political disillusionment; and at every stage there were non-kingly offices, especially that of "prophet," which assessed political performances from an independent covenantal standpoint. Gradually God's people began to hope that the Lord would send a ruler whose reign would not be

marred by lapses or disappointments. Increasingly this hope
took on a strong "eschatological" character—as in the beautiful
expression of this expectation in Isaiah 9:

> For to us a child is born,
> to us a son is given;
> and the government will be upon his shoulder,
> and his name will be called
> "Wonderful Counselor, Mighty God,
> Everlasting Father, Prince of Peace."
> Of the increase of his government and of peace
> there will be no end. (vv. 6-7)

This hasty sketch should provide us with enough evidence
to see that, in a sense, the political experience of God's people had come full circle. In the days of Saul, Israel had "rejected God from being king over them." But after a long series
of political disillusionments, God's people began to nourish
a political hope which could only be properly satisfied by God
himself, by a ruler who is not only the Wonderful Counselor
and the Prince of Peace, but is also the Mighty God and the
Everlasting Father.

Isaiah was especially sensitive to the tensions between the
present patterns of political wickedness and the promise of a
righteous ruler. As he observed comtemporary political life, he
saw nothing but corruption:

> The way of peace they know not,
> and there is no justice in their paths;
> they have made their roads crooked,
> no one who goes in them knows peace.
> Therefore justice is far from us,
> and righteousness does not overtake us. (59:8-9)

But someday

> a throne will be established in steadfast love
> and on it will sit in faithfulness
> in the tent of David
> one who judges and seeks justice
> and is swift to do righteousness. (16:5)

These passages illustrate the way in which the process has
come full circle—from having a divine king, to desiring a

human king, back to hoping for a divine king. But this is not a *mere* circle, because the political hope Isaiah expresses is, we might say, a post-human-king hope, not a pre-human-king one. Here is no mere return to a "primitive" theocracy. Isaiah's hope has been shaped by the historical-political process: the desire for the-king-greater-than-David is not merely the desire for the-king-before-Saul. God has used the political experience of his people to enrich and expand the human understanding of divine rule. Thus, once again, the fulfillment which God brings to his creation takes historical development into account.

But political fulfillment must also touch the lives of all of the nations of the world. God will not simply send a righteous ruler to his own people and leave it at that. There must be a general political accounting, a gathering-in of political authority.

God told the first human pair to exercise dominion together over the rest of the creation. But after their rebellion, God told the woman that she would be ruled by the man (Gen. 3:16)—thus began the patterns of the sinful domination of one human by another. Political authority quickly becomes institution-alized, and the structures of power are characterized by mani-pulation and deception, by injustice and unrighteousness.

The ways of human government in a sinful world are per-versions of the "subduing" and "dominion" which God in-tended as a part of the good creation. The curse of sin touches thrones and principalities, constitutions and legal systems. Tyranny, oppression, and manipulation are distortions of the good administrative patterns which God originally willed for his human creatures.

This wicked situation must be corrected, and it will be rec-tified in God's transformed City. Over and over again the Scriptures make this plain: the political power which has been so corrupted and twisted in the hands and hearts of sinful rulers must be returned to its rightful source. There must be a general political reckoning in which those who have misused the authority which comes from God alone acknowledge their error and rebellion. The righteous rule of God must achieve public vindication.

Therefore, people from many nations will enter the trans-formed City, "with their kings led in procession" (Isa. 60:11). God's people will someday "take captive those who were their

captors, and rule over those who oppressed them'' (Isa. 14:2)—
and ''the sons of those who oppressed you shall come bending low to you'' (Isa. 60:14). The nations of the earth will someday turn to the God of Jacob and ask him to ''judge between
the nations and . . . decide for many peoples'' (Isa. 2:4). This
notion of handing back political power to God is also found
in Paul's writings: the knees of those who have ruled ''on
earth'' will someday bow before Jesus, to the glory of the Father
(Phil. 2:11), for Jesus has ''disarmed the principalities and
powers and made a public example of them'' (Col. 2:15).

Isaiah's vision of the transformed City takes these elements
into account: a political reckoning must occur, and the power
that has been misused in political history must be handed back
to its proper source. And this must be in some sense a ''public''
event. The corrupt rulers of history must stand trial—the
unrighteous kings of Israel and Judah, the Egyptian pharaohs,
the rulers of Assyria and Syria, the Roman caesars, Hitler,
Stalin, Idi Amin, the corrupt politicians of the so-called ''free
world.'' Their abuses of power cannot go unchecked in the
final settling of accounts.

All of this, I hope, helps to make it clear why Isaiah and
John are not picturing these kings here as individual believers
who just happen to be politicians. The kings of the earth are
the bearers of ''the wealth of the nations.'' But they are also
officials who have held political power, a power rooted in the
will of God for his good creation. In the end time there must
be an accounting of the ways in which this power has been
used in human history, a transaction which requires the
presence of kings in the Holy City. And the transaction would
not be properly expedited if, say, only ''saved'' politicians were
allowed into the City.

But this raises a host of nitty-gritty questions. How long
will these politicians—at least the ''unsaved'' ones—stay in the
City? Will all of the rulers who have ever lived be paraded
through the City's streets? Are we actually to picture Adolf
Hitler as walking into the New Jerusalem—with, say, Anne
Frank and Dietrich Bonhoeffer leading him ''in procession''?

Needless to say, we have no biblical basis for answering
these questions specifically, and it would probably be wrong
to speculate too much here. A number of different scenarios

would seem to be compatible with Isaiah's account. It might be, for example, that the City will be visited only by a representation of kings—a sampling of rulers whose careers were characterized by various degrees of righteousness and unrighteousness.

But Isaiah does seem to be pointing to a *judging* of political history that will take place in the Holy City. A similar expectation is expressed in Revelation 6:9-11. There the martyred saints who have been slain for the sake of the Gospel cry out to the Lord, " 'How long before thou wilt judge and avenge our blood on those who dwell upon the earth?' " And they are advised "to rest a little longer," until the number of the martyrs is complete.

Christians who have suffered political persecution are not wrong in expecting some sort of accounting. The record will be put straight. As the Apostle Peter puts it, those who presently accuse Christians of being "wrongdoers" will "see your good deeds and glorify God on the day of visitation" (I Pet. 2:12). These New Testament passages, along with the references in Isaiah 60, suggest the real possibility that those believers who have been unjustly accused and punished by wicked rulers will be vindicated in the presence of their former accusers. If this interpretation is correct, then it is important that unjust rulers be brought into the City, not as permanent residents but as participants in a political reckoning.

It may also be that this reckoning will require that *non*-Christian victims appear in the City. But their entrance will have nothing to do with permanent residence in the city which God is preparing for his people; rather, it will have to do with debts which must be settled with respect to the persecution of non-Christians by non-Christians.

Two other possible encounters in the City must also be mentioned. One is a judging of the wicked deeds which Christian rulers have perpetrated against non-Christians. The other—and surely this is the most poignant and soul-wrenching kind of confrontation which we can imagine taking place on the streets of the Holy City—is the encounter between oppressed Christians and their Christian oppressors. Will there not be a very special and profound sadness that falls over the

City when the accounts must finally be settled between the Catholics and Protestants of Ireland, between Mennonite martyrs and their Calvinist persecutors, between the Christian plantation owner and his Christian slaves? In imagining what these kinds of meetings will be like, we can only trust in the biblical promise that God himself will wipe the tears away from the eyes of his children.

Thus the sins that have been committed in political history will be publicly exposed in the Holy City. God will not allow such wickedness to go unavenged. Political dictators will be led into the presence of those whom they have cast into prisons. Kings and queens will bow low before the widows and orphans whom they have oppressed. Cruel tyrants will hear the testimonies of those whom they have martyred. White racist politicians will wither under the gazes of black children.

And the Lord alone will be exalted in that day. The oppressive relationships which have occurred in sinful history will undergo no simple reversal in the transformed City. No attempt will be made to satisfy our more primitive yearnings for ''revenge.'' The goal of this vast and complex political reckoning will be the glorification of God, the universal recognition that the Lord alone is righteous in his verdicts and swift to do justice. God alone will judge between the nations and decide for many peoples in that final day of reckoning.

This political transaction which we have been discussing has the feel of an ''episode.'' It is something that will ''happen,'' and then it will be over. In reading the accounts of Isaiah and John, I do not get the sense that they are describing something that will be a permanent part of the scenery of the Holy City. The kings of the earth will not be marched through the streets of the City for ever and ever. All of this seems to be a part of the closing-off of sinful history; it is—if you wish—an episode in the mopping-up process.

The political reckoning—if it is an episode—will be followed by the instituting of the new order of life in the Eternal City. But when the Bible talks about the eternal order of things which will characterize the renewed creation, it does not speak of a completely ''a-political'' situation. The political disillusionment and suffering which God's people experience in history does not lead them to yearn for the elimination of politics; rather, they hope for a new *kind* of politics, a political transformation. Thus, in chapter 1, Isaiah views political fulfillment in these terms:

> Therefore the Lord says,
> the Lord of hosts,
> the Mighty One of Israel:
> "Ah, I will vent my wrath on my enemies,
> and avenge myself on my foes.
> I will turn my hand against you
> and will smelt away your dross as with lye
> and remove all your alloy.
> And I will restore your judges as at the first,
> and your counselors as at the beginning.
> Afterward you shall be called the city of righteousness,
> the faithful city." (vv. 24-26)

The best of the political past, then, will be restored in the glorious future—righteous counselors and judges will be restored "as at the beginning." In Isaiah 60 the language of "rule" is retained in describing the transformed City, but it is very different from the political rule that prevails under sinful conditions: "I will make your overseers peace and your taskmasters righteousness" (v. 17). Peace and righteousness themselves will administer the affairs of the City. The book of Revelation also retains the language of governance, introducing the notion of human dominion under the power of God's throne: "and his servants shall worship him . . . and they shall reign for ever and ever" (Rev. 22:3-5).

Political authority, then, will be healed and sanctified in the end time. John describes the leaves of the tree which stands in the City as bringing about "the healing of the nations" (Rev. 22:2)—and there is every reason to expect that this includes *political* healing.

Two of Isaiah's images in chapter 60 are important for our understanding of the healing and sanctification of politics. In verse 10 he tells us that the kings of the earth—like the rams of Nebaioth—will "minister" to the people of God. And in verse 16 he portrays God's people as "sucking the breast of kings."

The "ministry" image can be tied to a number of biblical themes. Just as the vessels and goods of commercial activity will be stripped of idolatrous associations, so the patterns of political rule will be restored to their proper function of "servanthood" in human affairs. Nor can we ignore the obvious parallel here to Paul's teaching in Romans 13:6, that the political "authorities are ministers of God." There are a number of possible interpretations of this passage, but the most plausible seems to be that Paul is describing political authority as it *ought* to function. A properly functioning government will be "God's servant for good," his "minister" (Rom. 13:4, 6). It is the restoration of this good function of government which Isaiah is envisioning in his description of the City.

This is not the place to discuss at length the proper functioning of government. But referring to this topic in passing should not leave the impression that it is a subject that can be dealt with in a facile manner. Christians must have a complex perspective on government, because we recognize the complexities of a world that is not only created but fallen, and not only fallen but in the process of being rescued by God's redeeming work.

The kind of government or rule which might be necessary in an unfallen world will differ in important ways from the patterns of political authority which emerge under sinful conditions. In a rebellious world, coercive governments, invested with the power of the sword, are necessary. They are, in an important sense, a curb on human wickedness, a divinely ordained remedy for our fallenness.

This is a matter which Christian people have often stressed, an emphasis grounded in biblical teaching. Coercive governments introduce a necessary "order" into the corporate life of a fallen humanity. In restraining sin in a rebellious world, coercive governments "minister" to us.

The Christian Church has seldom run the risk of denying this important biblical emphasis on "order." But Christian people have often shown a serious insensitivity to the implications of an equally significant biblical truth—that governments are not merely a response *to* sin, but are also affected *by* sin. Governments can become "beastly," can function as objects of idolatrous designs. They can—even in the name of "law and order"—commit themselves to injustice, unrighteousness, and oppression. They often perpetuate the legal and economic helplessness of the widow, the orphan, and the sojourner. They glory in their own military prowess. They initiate imperialist and genocidal programs. Sometimes they grow weak and ineffective. In pursuing selfish goals and policies they are no longer "ministers" of the Lord, and their behavior cannot be justified by pious platitudes about "life in a sinful world." Such governments stand under the stern judgment of God.

A good government, stripped of its rebellious and idolatrous designs, will serve and nurture its citizens—thus the "breast" image of verse 16 in Isaiah's account. If there were no other reason to take note of this image, it would be necessary in the light of current sensitivities to "sex-role stereotyping." The language of authority and rule has often been heavily weighted with "male," "military" associations. The Old Testament itself, with its strong patriarchal imagery, regularly exhibits this pattern. The use of this image, then, is a pleasant surprise: kings who have their own breast-milk to offer! The God who is both king and nurturer will in the end time bring milk from "the breast of kings." Politics will become a force for the giving of life. King-mothers will feed the people of God.

Earlier I noted that when God's people became disillusioned with human political rulers, they began to hope for a divine rule which would be characterized by an unfailing justice and righteousness and peace. I also noted that this hope for divine rule gradually began to be expressed in terms of an expectation of a divine *person*—the "Wonderful Counselor" of Isaiah 9.

Christians today have an advantage over Isaiah. We have learned the name of the nurturing ruler: "Jesus Christ the faithful witness, the first-born of the dead, and the ruler of kings on earth" (Rev. 1:5). Jesus is the king who, when he stood over the rebellious city of Jerusalem, longed to gather her as a mother hen gathers her little ones under her wings. He is the shepherd-ruler who carries his lambs in his bosom, and gently leads those who are with young.

In describing his vision of the transformed City, Isaiah prophesies the coming of a new political *order*; he spells out the shape of this order in only the most general terms. Kings will be transformed into nurturers and ministers. Peace itself will become an overseer, and Righteousness itself a taskmaster. But, as we have just noted, in his book of prophecies Isaiah sometimes gives this order a more *personal* focus. The promise of political transformation must be embodied in a specific ruler, one who will spring forth from "the root of Jesse" and will "stand as an ensign to the peoples" (11:10).

In the New Testament this ensign appears when God assumes human flesh and dies on the Cross to liberate his creation. For Christians the anticipation of the new political order must take the shape of obedience to the rule of Jesus Christ. In our life together as the blood-bought people of God we must live in the knowledge of his "political" instructions to his disciples:

> "You know that the rulers of the Gentiles lord it over them, and their great men exercise authority over them. It shall not be so among you; but whoever would be great among you must be your servant, and whoever would be first among you must be your slave; even as the Son of man came not to be served but to serve, and to give his life as a ransom for many." (Matt. 20:25-28)

Jesus has already begun to transform the patterns of human authority. He calls us to cast our lot with the lowly ones, to identify with the poor and the oppressed of the earth. To live in this manner is to anticipate the coming political vindication, when "the least one shall become a clan, and the smallest one a mighty nation" (Isa. 60:22).

In many ways the promise of political sanctification is a mysterious, and even a baffling, notion. But it is also true that in many ways it is a very encouraging promise for us in the present age. For one thing, we can act politically in the full assurance that our political deeds will count toward the day of reckoning that will occur in the transformed City. This vision of the political future is not one which should inspire us to be politically passive. In his second epistle, Peter tells Christians to "maintain good conduct among the Gentiles," even though we may be labeled "wrongdoers" by those who perpetuate the status quo; the important thing is not that we blend into the present political landscape, but that our accusers see our "good deeds and glorify God on the day of visitation" (I Pet. 2:12). This is one important sense in which present acts will "count" in the future Day.

Since we are already citizens of God's commonwealth, we must find effective ways of living in political conformity to its norms and patterns. Because we know that all political rulers will someday be called to account before the only true Sovereign, we must not give them more than their due in the present age. And from the perspective of the New Testament, what is "due" them is not blind obedience or uncritical submission—and it certainly is not worship or idolatrous trust. What we must show present-day political authority is honor, because we recognize that it is called to perform an important ministry. But as those who know the radicality of the sin which presently affects both individuals and structures, we can only properly "honor" political authority today by constantly calling it to perform that kind of ministry which God requires of all who administer human affairs.

Those of us who have learned the name of God's anointed ruler must never despair concerning the basic political patterns which are a part of the "filling" of the creation. The Savior who presently calls his disciples to obedient servanthood is also the one before whom every ruler will someday bow. And he is the one who will someday address the creation with words of political healing. On that day all flesh will see that he is—in a profoundly political sense—a Wonderful Counselor.

The Milk
of
Many Nations

There are several ways in which people appeal to the Old Testament in order to justify and reinforce racial prejudice. One way is using the "curse of Ham" incident as a basis for arguing that black people deserve to be kept in a subservient position. A second way is appealing to the story of the Tower of Babel as a rationale for policies of "racial separation."

In 1974 the white Dutch Reformed Church of South Africa adopted a report entitled *Human Relations and the South African Scene in the Light of Scripture.* This report rejects in no uncertain terms the "curse of Ham" ideology as a confused and even perverse reading of the Bible. But it does make extensive use of the Babel incident as a reason for its qualified endorsement of the policy of "separate development" in South African society. As a result of Babel, the report argues, God introduces "distinctions among peoples" into the human race. Ethnic "diversity," then, is not a bad thing, and "the church should avoid the modern tendency to erase all distinctions among peoples." Rather, Christians should point to the love of neighbor as "the ethical norm for the regulation of relationships among peoples."

A third way in which people defend "racial separation" on Old Testament grounds is more subtle. Many national and ethnic groups tend to identify themselves with the "chosen people" of the Old Testament. The New England Puritans identified themselves as chosen, and the conviction still flavors many popular celebrations of "Americanism." This notion also shapes the thinking of the English, the Scots, the Dutch, and other national and ethnic groups.

While reading James Michener's powerful novel *The Covenant,* I was struck by the manner in which the Old Testament shaped the life and thought of South Africa's Afrikaners. Indeed, each of these three Old Testament elements played an important role in the self-understanding of this white South African group. They viewed themselves as God's chosen people, sent into the wilderness to build the commonwealth of Zion. To them, the dark-skinned inhabitants of that land were an accursed people—the ''Canaanites''—whose destiny it was to serve the white community as ''your hewers of wood and your drawers of water.'' And underlying this conviction was the assumption that the Lord had ordained the separation of the races.

In clear contrast to the Afrikaners and their Old Testament orientation, the white English-speaking people who settled in South Africa were much more inclined—as Michener portrays them—to think in New Testament terms. For them the Christian Church was a community of the Gentiles in which the ethnocentric patterns of the Old Testament had been set aside. In the Body of Christ the barriers which have separated peoples had to be broken down.

Michener's portrayal of the differences between these two groups makes much of their respective loyalties to the Old and New Testaments. And there is much to be said for this portrayal, both as an analysis of the differences in racial attitudes between these two groups and as a general theological comment on the differences between the Old and New Testaments. But as a point of theology (which is not, of course, Michener's primary concern), it is only roughly true.

It is sometimes said that in the Old Testament salvation is for the Jews, whereas in the New Testament the offer of redemption is extended to people from all nations. And in very general terms, this is accurate. But it does fail to take into account some subtleties in Old Testament thought. Already in the older Testament we find hints of an opening-up of the redemptive mercies of God to peoples of all nations.

Strong hints of this sort are found in Isaiah's writings, especially in Isaiah 60. Isaiah pictures the Holy City as a meeting-place for the nations of the earth. Artifacts and goods from many nations are carried into the City, and the kings of many nations are brought into the City for a political reckoning. But Isaiah's interest in multi-national diversity is not limited to the treatment of cultural instruments and political office-holders. There is also to be a gathering of the common citizenry of the nations of the earth—ordinary *people* will be gathered together. Sons and daughters will travel to the City "from afar" (v. 4). Foreigners will build up the City's walls (v. 10). The kings will be led into the City by people who have been their subjects (v. 11). And the multi-national complexion of the eternal commonwealth will be a *nurturing* force in the life of God's people: "You shall suck the milk of nations" (v. 16).

It is possible that Isaiah thought of some of these people who come to the City from many nations as Jewish people who had been dispersed into other countries. It is also possible that the "foreigners" who will work on the walls of the renewed Jerusalem are people who were once oppressors of the Jews. But these two categories do not seem to exhaust Isaiah's meaning here; he also makes what seems to be a more expansive reference to people from other nations. He indicates that non-Hebrew peoples will actually receive the benefits of God's redemption, that they will be drawn to the light of the City in a spirit of rejoicing: "Nations will come to your light" (v. 3). Foreigners will enter victoriously into the City, leading their kings "in procession" (v. 11). This strongly suggests that Jew and Gentile alike will be included in the redeemed company, to enjoy the benefits of "the milk of nations."

This suggestion takes on a more distinct shape when we consider what Isaiah writes elsewhere in his book of prophecy. In chapter 2 he articulates the promise that the Lord will "decide for many peoples" on the day when "all the nations shall flow" to the Lord's mountain, requesting that they be taught to walk in his ways (vv. 2-4). Similarly, in chapter 14 Isaiah predicts that "aliens will join [Israel] and will cleave to the house of Jacob" (v. 1). And in chapter 25 he sees a day coming when "the Lord of hosts will make for all peoples a feast of fat things," and "the veil that is spread over all nations" will be forever removed (vv. 6-7).

Isaiah's most explicit and extensive reference to this matter is found in chapter 19, which is worth quoting at length:

In that day there will be an altar to the Lord in the midst of the land of Egypt, and a pillar to the Lord at its border. It will be a sign and a witness to the Lord of hosts in the land of Egypt; when they cry to the Lord because of oppressors he will send them a savior, and will defend and deliver them. And the Lord will make himself known to the Egyptians; and the Egyptians will know the Lord in that day and worship with sacrifice and burnt offering, and they will make vows to the Lord and perform them. And the Lord will smite Egypt, smiting and healing, and they will return to the Lord, and he will heed their supplications and heal them. In that day there will be a highway from Egypt to Assyria, and the Assyrian will come into Egypt, and the Egyptian into Assyria, and the Egyptians will worship with the Assyrians. In that day Israel will be the third with Egypt and Assyria, a blessing in the midst of the earth, whom the Lord of hosts has blessed, saying, "Blessed be Egypt my people, and Assyria the work of my hands, and Israel my heritage." (vv. 19-25)

It is difficult to see how Isaiah could have thought about the events which he describes here without sensing that he was standing before a great mystery. So much of Old Testament thinking rests on the premise that the Hebrew people are God's unique covenant-partners and that all other nations are the Lord's permanent enemies. Isaiah himself regularly follows this pattern of thought. Furthermore, there were good historical reasons why the Hebrews viewed Egypt and Assyria as very special enemies. And yet Isaiah articulates the almost unthinkable thought that God would someday call Egypt "my people" and Assyria "the work of my hands"—phrases which elsewhere are consistently applied to the citizens of Israel and Judah.

The ethnocentrism of the Old Testament is not a matter which we ought to treat condescendingly. In the divine redemptive economy of the Old Testament, God did choose to single out a specific people, the children of Jacob, as the special object of his covenantal care. The unique status of the Hebrew people, then, was not a figment of their own prideful imaginations; it was based on the sovereign good pleasure of God. The Lord chose to initiate his redemptive plan by focusing on a single ethnic nation; and the promise to do so was first given to Abraham, a promise confirmed in the Exodus and given special structure on Mount Sinai.

This plan must be viewed, in turn, against the backdrop of the confusion of tongues at Babel. Because of human rebellion God saw fit to introduce linguistic, ethnic, and national boundaries into the human community. And his plan of salvation in the Old Testament was worked out within this framework. Thus God chose a particular people as the special object of his love and care.

The earthly ministry of the divine-human person Jesus also took place within the Hebrew community. Indeed, some of Jesus' closest disciples strongly resisted the "de-Judaizing" process in the life of the early church. Pentecost, however, was a landmark event in this regard. There the judgment on Babel was lifted:

> And they were amazed and wondered, saying, "Are not all these who are speaking Galileans? And how is it that we hear, each of us in his own native language? Parthians and Medes and Elamites and residents of Mesopotamia, Judea and Cappadocia, Pontus and Asia, Phrygia and Pamphylia, Egypt and the parts of Libya belonging to Cyrene, and visitors from Rome, both Jews and proselytes, Cretans and Arabians, we hear them telling in our own tongues the mighty works of God." (Acts 2:7-11)

Peter realized the implications of Pentecost when he visited the home of Cornelius: " 'Truly I perceive that God shows no partiality, but in every nation any one who fears him and does what is right is acceptable to him' " (Acts 10:34). This same theme is celebrated in Paul's announcement that in Christ Jesus "there is neither Jew nor Greek . . . and if you are Christ's, then you are Abraham's offspring, heirs according to promise" (Gal. 3:28-29).

To be sure, patterns of an opening-up to the Gentiles were already developing during Old Testament times. The Hebrew people did engage in a limited evangelistic outreach to other nations. Some "strangers in the land" became Jews; outsiders were incorporated into the house of Jacob by marriage—as in the case of Ruth the Moabite. The dispersion put God's people into daily contact with "foreigners"—and the mere

presence of Hebrew communities in other nations contributed
to the "internationalizing" of Judaism. So there was, in a
limited sense, a gathering-in of the nations in the Old Testament. But it was difficult to think of this process, within the
Old Testament framework, as anything but a "Judaizing" of
people from other nations. Reconciliation with God required
incorporation into the life of the Jewish people.

When Isaiah looks into the future, however, he seems to
discern the outline of a different pattern—a redemptive plan
which no longer centers exclusively on the Jewish people. John,
in turn, has a very clear grasp of this new arrangement. Like
Isaiah, he acknowledges—in Revelation 21:24—that in the City
"the nations" will walk in God's light. And in John's account
all traces of a Hebrew-centered religion are erased.

The multi-national character of the redeemed community
is announced with great fanfare in Revelation 5. No one is
found—either in the heavenly regions or on earth or in the sub-
terranean realm—who is worthy to open the scroll which contains the secrets of history. John weeps over this fact. Then
suddenly the announcement is made that a worthy person has
been found, a person described in decidedly Jewish terms: he
is "the Lion of the tribe of Judah" and of "the root of David."
But the one who appears is neither very lion-like nor very
Jewish. The one who steps forth to open the scroll is the Lamb
to whom a "new song" is sung:

> "Worthy art thou to take the scroll and to open its seals,
> for thou wast slain and by thy blood didst ransom men
>   for God
> from every tribe and tongue and people and nation,
> and hast made them a kingdom and priests to our
>   God. . . ." (vv. 9-10)

It is not difficult to understand why this is referred to as
a "new song," even though its message was foretold in ancient times. The foundation of the new peoplehood described
here is the redemptive sacrifice of Jesus, who is the Lamb without blemish. The shedding of his blood initiates a new covenant which extends far beyond the borders of Judaism. The
new community whose very existence rests on this founda-

tion is drawn from "every tribe and tongue and people and nation."

And this peoplehood, as described here in Revelation, now functions as both "kingdom" and "priests"—thus John employs both political and cultic language. People from every nation will be molded into a new "political" unit, a kingdom. All other patterns of organizing people into national, ethnic, and linguistic groups will have faded away. No longer will human "blood" have any status in evaluating and organizing people; only the blood of the Lamb is relevant here—thus providing a new basis for human unity. The God who once created all human beings out of one human blood is now reuniting them on the basis of the one Blood of Jesus.

The new community of the people of God is also a group of "priests." Because of the mediatorial work of the Lamb, there is no longer any need for certain human beings to serve as a special group of mediating cultic figures. Each citizen of the new community has direct access to God. And cultic rites of purification are no longer necessary, since each individual is forever made pure by the blood of Christ.

In the Eternal City, then, individuals drawn from every nation will be formed into a new community. The citizens of this City will be given golden crowns and purified robes so that all may participate in the everlasting rule of the saints as kings and priests.

The contrast between the religious life of the Old Testament and the patterns of the Eternal City is important to keep in mind. Hebrew religion centered on an ethnic people whose political and religious life was governed by an elite caste of kings and priests. In the Eternal City the ethnic basis is removed and people from many nations serve together—all of them—as kings and priests.

The "new song," then, highlights the culmination of the significant transition between the ancient ways of the Hebrews and the transformed patterns of the Heavenly City. Some commentators on this passage in Revelation 5 have dwelt on the fact that John expected to see a Lion, only to witness the appearance of a Lamb. This has been especially important to Christians in the "peace church" tradition, who see this as a challenge to sinful concepts of "power" and "victory." Certainly much in that idea invites reflection. But it is equally important that John was led to expect *Judah's* Lion, but that the Lamb who appears is the creator of a *multi-national* community.

The church that was founded at Pentecost, and as it exists today, stands between the Old Testament age and the coming manifestation of the eternal order of things. Though the old ethnocentric ways of the Hebrews have been put behind us, the fully transformed City has not yet appeared. We are, however, seeing present signs of the fulfillment of Isaiah's prophecy in our midst.

I once spoke to a group of people in my own predominantly Dutch denomination about applying Isaiah's prophecy to our denominational life. This denomination has a small but increasing number of black, Hispanic, Native Indian, and Oriental members and congregations. On the basis of Isaiah 60, I argued that this multi-ethnic phenomenon was a fulfillment of prophecy—in our own denomination many nations and peoples were being gathered into the City. As our discussion proceeded I became aware of the image which some of my fellow church-members were entertaining as they listened to what I said; and it was an image that I had subtly encouraged by my own way of presenting the topic. We were thinking of ourselves, Dutch-American Calvinists, as the occupants of the City, and we were envisioning the "foreigners"—black, red, yellow, and brown—as entering into the City presently occupied by us white folks. To be sure, the people in this group were pleased by this gathering-in; but we were still picturing the situation as one in which "they" were entering "our" city.

Now, as a matter of sociological fact, this is a fairly accurate portrayal of how things are happening in my denomination. We are a very white—even Dutch—"city"; and "they" have begun to enter into the city as new citizens. But this will not do as a theological account of what is happening in *the* City, the community which God is preparing for his people. *That* City began as a Jewish center, and now, in the New Testament dispensation, the "foreigners" are entering in. And we are *all* (except, perhaps, for Christian Jews) "the foreigners." All of us—Dutch, Irish, Italian, Black, Hispanic, Navajo, Chinese—

are entering into the City which God has transformed from a Jewish center into a multi-national center. We—all of us as Gentile Christians—are the foreigners being welcomed into God's City.

"Red and yellow, black and white, they are precious in his sight." These words from the children's song express a profound biblical truth. God's redeeming love reaches out to people from all tribes and nations. God was not satisfied to limit his covenant promises to the Hebrew people; he has called many nations to come and dwell in his City. And this has been his plan even from the ancient times, when he said to his prophet:

> "It is too light a thing that you should be my servant
> to raise up the tribes of Jacob
> and to restore the preserved of Israel;
> I will give you as a light to the nations,
> that my salvation may reach to the end of the earth."
> (Isa. 49:6)

But *why* is this so? Can we perceive some divine motif underlying the multi-national purposes of God as he gathers the redeemed into the City? One of the more fascinating proposals which has been made in theological discussions of the biblical notion of "the image of God" is that this image has a "corporate" dimension. That is, there is no one human individual or group who can fully bear or manifest all that is involved in the image of God, so that there is a sense in which that image is collectively possessed. The image of God is, as it were, parceled out among the peoples of the earth. By looking at different individuals and groups we get glimpses of different aspects of the full image of God.

We do not need to examine this suggestion carefully as a technical proposal concerning the meaning of the phrase "image of God." But we can note that there is at least something about the *spirit* of this suggestion which does have biblical grounding. Both Isaiah and John view the nations as bringing their "wealth," their "honor and glory," into the City. Surely this is meant to point to the diversity of riches distributed across the nations—riches not limited to material possessions.

The racial, ethnic, and national diversity of the human race exhibits many differences in character traits, temperaments, and cultural patterns. Admittedly, this notion has often been expressed in terms of misleading—even wicked—"stereotypes," which have been sinful vehicles for bearing false witness against our neighbors. Nevertheless, by God's providence different peoples have lived in different geographical settings and climates, and the human spirit has cultivated diverse social, political, and economic conditions. Physical distances and natural barriers have thus given rise to valuable alternative patterns of social development.

Here we must face a seeming paradox in the biblical story. On the one hand the "scattering" of the peoples of the earth—as in the Babel account—seems to have been caused by human sin. It is in a sense a divine punishment for our corporate rebellion. But at the same time the resulting linguistic, national, racial, and geographical barriers have stimulated the development of diverse gifts and talents among humankind.

Once again it must be noted that God takes historical development into account. In one very important sense, it would seem, God's decision at Babel to scatter the peoples was for him a regrettable one. It was a necessary response to human rebellion, but historical development moved along very different lines than it would have if sin had not entered human affairs.

This does not mean, however, that the sinful development of humankind has produced no good. Indeed, linguistic, racial, and national boundaries have provided the framework for a variety of cultural and social experiments involving the human spirit. When the end of history arrives, then, there *is* something to be gathered in—diverse cultural riches to be brought into the Heavenly City. That which has been parceled out in human history must now be collected for the glory of the creator.

As already noted, Isaiah once again uses a nurturing image to describe the benefits that God's people will receive from the multi-national life of the City: they will "suck the milk of nations." The citizens of the renewed Jerusalem will be "fed" by the presence of many peoples bearing diverse gifts. "Red and yellow, black and white"—and all that these labels designate—will be precious to God and to all of his saints.

Not long ago a white South African clergyman was sent by his denomination to conduct a worship service, which included the celebration of the Lord's Supper, in an outlying area. A group of soldiers from the South African army attended this service. One of the soldiers was a young man of mixed race, officially classified as "Coloured" under South Africa's racial laws. The visiting clergyman refused to conduct the service until this young man left. When the clergyman was later asked how he could defend refusing to serve communion to a fellow citizen who was serving his country, he replied: "Since when is he a fellow citizen? He is not that."

This clergyman's answer is not far from the truth when taken as a technical point about the legal status of black and brown persons in South Africa. But his theology is sadly defective. If they are followers of Jesus Christ, the white clergyman and the brown soldier are already fellow citizens in that holy commonwealth which will someday be a gathered community in the Holy City. In the present age, even prior to the appearance of the City, this common citizenship is profoundly important.

Indeed, Isaiah's prophecy about the Holy City can be thought of as having a three-stage fulfillment. The renewal of Jerusalem occurred in very partial and fragmentary ways already in the Old Testament, when certain dispersed Jews returned to their homeland. A second stage of fulfillment occurred in the life of the New Testament church: already in the New Testament period the "nations" began to be gathered into the community of God's people. And this gathering-in, which continues to occur today, is an important preparation for the appearance of the Eternal City, where the full splendor of the nations will be received into God's commonwealth.

So the white South African clergyman who looked out at his congregation and saw a brown face there ought to have rejoiced over the fulfillment of prophecy which he was witnessing. Indeed, the fact that this kind of gathering-in of peoples was occurring in a social environment hostile to the "mixing" of the races should only have added to his joy.

I once heard a story of another clergyman who had to face the issue of racial integration at a communion service. This young pastor was called to serve an all-white congregation in an area of the United States where the patterns of overt racial prejudice were still deeply entrenched. At the beginning of his pastorate in that congregation he made a vow to the Lord that he would gently but firmly prepare the people for the time— and he carefully charted the schedule in his own mind—when he would speak to them about what the Gospel demands of race relations.

But his own carefully orchestrated timetable was interrupted one "communion Sunday" when a group of black Christians walked into the service and sat in the front pew. The young pastor observed that the lay leaders of the congregation had approached the blacks and were asking them to leave. Surveying the situation, he went to the communion table and picked up a tray of bread. Then he walked over to the black visitors and extended the tray to them, with these words: "The body of Christ was broken for you."

This man realized that God was using these black visitors to interrupt his own pastoral schedule. In that tense moment he had no other choice but to make the demands of the Gospel clear to his congregation. To fail to do so would have meant disobedience to the heavenly vision. For the Lord's Supper is an anticipation of the day when the Lord himself will prepare "for all peoples a feast of fat things." In the church today "the veil that is spread over all nations" is already being lifted. At the very least, then, Christians should actively work to abolish patterns of ethnic and racial discrimination *within* the Christian community. We ought to look for new and better ways to "suck the milk of nations" in our life together as the people of God.

The way in which the case is put here may raise questions in some people's minds. Does this mean that we ought to be more concerned about discrimination against Christians than against non-Christians? Is there not a very basic sense in which "human rights" are grounded in the fact that all human beings—regardless of whether or not they are Christians—are created by God?

There is a venerable tradition of appealing to "creation" as a basis for treating every person as free and equal. In the United States this tradition is expressed in the declaration that human beings "are endowed by their Creator with certain unalienable rights''—an emphasis that is paralleled by Protestant liberalism's teachings regarding ''the Fatherhood of God and the Brotherhood of Man.''

It would be difficult to argue that this emphasis is completely misguided. The Bible does teach that all human beings are created in God's image, a fact which has profound implications about the way in which human beings *as* human beings ought to be viewed and treated. But I do think that it is, in important ways, an inadequate basis for opposing patterns of discrimination.

A few years ago I was asked to draft a letter that I and some of my faculty colleagues wanted to send to a group of white Christian academics in South Africa. A series of especially distressing events had just occurred in South Africa—the most despicable being the murder of Steve Biko by representatives of the government—and we wanted to encourage a prophetic response to this situation by our counterparts in that country. In writing the letter I quoted the King James version of Acts 17:26, which I had always thought of as a powerful statement on ''race relations'': God ''hath made of one blood all nations of men.'' Much to my dismay, I discovered later on that this text is a favorite of racist groups in South Africa, who point out that the verse goes on to note that the Lord ''hath determined . . . the bounds of their habitation''—a qualification that they view as justifying *apartheid* policies.

The racist use of this text does show, I think, that an appeal to the fact of God's creation of the human race is, in itself, inadequate to establish a basis for racial justice. The perpetuators of injustice can argue that God did indeed create all people out of ''one blood.'' But, they can go on to argue, sin has altered the original situation. In response to human rebellion, God has introduced (remembering the words of the report of the Dutch Reformed Church) ''distinctions among peoples.'' And what God has put asunder let no man try to join together!

The only effective way of countering this kind of theology, it seems to me, is to point to the work of the Cross. This does not mean that ''creation'' becomes irrelevant. But it does mean that it is not enough to appeal to the fact of creation without viewing it in the light of the work of redemption. We cannot ignore the Babel account or the provisional divisions of the race that God introduced in response to the pretensions of the tower-builders. But through Calvary and Pentecost God has begun to "lift the veil." In Jesus Christ the barriers of race and clan and tribe and tongue are being abolished. Redemption restores the work of creation, and in doing so it also repairs the damage done by sin.

Thus I must repeat my earlier comment: at the very least, Christians should actively work to abolish patterns of ethnic and racial discrimination *within* the Christian community. But what does "at the very least" mean? Does it mean that Christians should not be as concerned about racial injustice outside the Christian community as they are with such practices within the Christian community? In a word, no. The redemptive work of Christ has rendered *all* patterns of segregation and apartheid illegitimate. Whoever discriminatory patterns oppress—black Baptists in the United States, Anglican Eskimos in Canada, Jews in the Soviet Union, Muslims in Palestine, Buddhists in Vietnam—we must voice our protest against the suffering caused by human labeling-systems which have now been transcended by the Cross of Christ.

In an important sense it should be (but isn't always!) *easier* to eliminate racial and ethnic prejudice within the Christian community. Wherever the victory of the Cross is clearly acknowledged, we can appeal directly to the cleansing power of the blood of Christ for racial and ethnic relations. But arguments based on a theology of atonement will be less than convincing where the redemptive work of Christ is not acknowledged. The illegitimacy of racial and ethnic distinctions should be clear, then, "at the very least" in the Christian community. But Christians must also recognize that the Cross remains normative even where its efficacy is not acknowledged. Thus the oppression of Jews by Marxists is no less sinful than the oppression of black Calvinists by white Calvinists. And Christian opposition to injustice can be no less decisive in one case than it is in the other.

The "at the very least" phrase may also help us set our priorities in some cases. While all oppression is wicked, we must often hold ourselves most accountable for the problems "closest to home." For the Christian, "home" is in a very important sense the Christian church—"elect from every nation, yet one o'er all the earth''—although ''home'' will also be our neighborhoods, our school districts, our voting precincts, our labor unions, and our shopping centers.

But we must care ''at the very least'' about the church because the Christian community ought to function as a model of, a pointer to, what life will be like in the Eternal City of God. The church must be, here and now, a place into which the peoples of the earth are being gathered for new life.

The Canons of Dort, a seventeenth-century Calvinist document, contain a marvelous phrase that applies here. The Canons say that the Gospel ''ought to be declared and published to all nations, promiscuously and without distinction.'' (Isn't it odd, then, that the white Dutch Reformed Church of South Africa, for whom these Canons are a creedal document, should talk so much about ''distinctions among people''?) This is one area of the Christian life where ''promiscuity'' is desirable. Just as a sexually licentious person chooses bed-partners without regard to marital woes or bonds of fidelity, so the Christian community ought to be promiscuous in inviting people, without regard for racial or ethnic or national identity, into the fellowship of God's redeemed people.

The examples I have cited in this discussion give the impression that I think that racial prejudice and ethnocentrism are problems only for white people—an impression that it would be wrong not to correct. Certain Oriental Christian groups have great difficulty accepting persons from other Oriental countries into their fellowship. The church on the African continent has had to struggle regularly with deeply ingrained patterns of ''tribalism.'' And the Meti people of Canada have suffered at the hands of Eskimos and Ojibways as well as whites. Wherever human beings are victimized by false pride and prejudices rooted in convictions about racial or tribal ''superiority,'' we are witnessing the ravages of sin.

But there is a somewhat different kind of ''ethnic pride'' which must be noted. In recent years we have seen an increasing emphasis on a sort of ''ethnic consciousness'' which has had an important impact on the life of the church. Black people, for example, have become aware of their own ''roots,'' and there has been much interest in the development of a ''black theology''—and a ''red theology,'' and various kinds of "third-world theologies." Don't these interests run counter to the emphasis here on eliminating such factors in the Christian community? Isn't this "ethnic consciousness" a perpetuation, in its own way, of an undue Christian attention to racial distinctions?

Not necessarily. In order to understand why, it is important to refer again to the fact that every tribe and nation will bring its "wealth," its unique cultural riches, into the transformed City. But it is a sad and obvious fact of human history that some peoples have been severely oppressed by others, and allowed to cultivate their talents only under tyrannical conditions.

The black peoples of North America and South Africa serve as important examples of this fact. In these societies black persons have systematically suffered under the yoke of racism, and the black family has been under sustained attack. Blacks have been treated as "sub-human" or "inferior" entities, as economic commodities to be bought and sold. Many factors—overt and covert, blatant and subtle—have combined to wage war on the black person's sense of self-worth.

Under such difficult conditions the black spirit has often provided us with examples of amazing courage and resilience. Spiritual riches have been mined from the depths of physical and cultural deprivation. Oppressed black peoples—*as* victims of oppression—have significant gifts which they will carry into the Heavenly City.

But there can be no doubt that, under the conditions just described—and these are only general inequities, not specific injustices—blacks have been severely restricted in developing their own "glory and honor." Because of this, we must view the "black consciousness" movement of recent years as an important expression of a renewed sense of dignity and self-worth. And "black theology" is a systematic attempt within the Christian community to articulate an understanding of the Gospel which is free from the "white" interests and priorities and illusions which have for so long shaped—in both obvious and subtle ways—the thinking, life, and witness of the Christian community.

"Black consciousness" can be an important kind of preparation for the entry of many peoples into the transformed City.

It is one significant exploration of "the glory and the honor of the nations" which will someday be received into the place which God has prepared for his people. It is a necessary program for guaranteeing that the cultural—and theological—wealth of the nations will not be dominated by the interests of the white oppressor.

This is one of those situations in which we can become less racially conscious only by becoming more conscious of the patterns of racial oppression. If "the glory and the honor" of white people is to be received into the transformed City, the patterns of white cultural life and theological reflection must be cleansed of the deep and long-standing influences of racism and imperialism. The "black consciousness" movement, and parallel phenomena in other cultural groups, must be viewed as a significant gift to the entire people of God, as we prepare together to live in the Holy City. It is a profound contribution to the process of the healing of the nations.

It is even possible—in my own thinking it is quite likely—that throughout eternity we will be aware of who we are and where we have come from—aware not only of our individual personality traits but also of our cultural, ethnic, and racial identities. It may be that the exchange of those cultural gifts which have been forged under the pressures of sinful historical development will not be a single event but an ongoing dialogue in the continuing life of the Heavenly City. Perhaps the fully sanctified *exploration* of "the glory and the honor of the nations" is a process that will only begin as we enter the gates of the City.

Perhaps. Once again, certain important dimensions of the life of the City remain shrouded in mystery. But there is no mystery about the basic fact that the gates of the commonwealth of God have been opened up to all peoples. The God who in ancient times called a specific ethnic people, the tribes of Israel, into a special relationship with himself has begun in these latter days to establish a "holy race" made up of people from every tribe and tongue and nation. The God of Israel has addressed the Xhosa as "my people" and has called Polish laborers "the works of my hands." Mexicans have become "Abraham's offspring," and Koreans have been named "heirs according to the promise." The Lord has assembled together

Scots and Swedes, Iranians and Navajos, and has addressed them, saying: "Once you were no-people, but now you are my-people."

Needless to say, there are important "strategy" questions which must be faced if we are to respond in obedience to this work of the Lord in the church today. Long-standing relationships of "dependency" must be broken. People who have known degradation and oppression must be liberated for the exciting Christian task of discovering "the glory and the honor" of the unique cultural gifts which the Lord has given them. New programs of congregational life and denominational organization and inter-congregational cooperation and cross-cultural exchange must be put into practice. Complex and sensitive issues must be honestly explored. Painful processes of healing must occur.

But the biblical message is clear. The blood of God's son has purchased a new peoplehood, a nation of kings and priests gathered from the ends of the earth. The rending of the veil in Jerusalem's temple has effected the lifting of the veil which has for so long covered the nations. We can begin to "suck the milk of nations."

Where Is
the Light
Coming From?

Many striking similarities exist between Isaiah's and John's visions of the Holy City. It is obvious that both men were "working with the same material." John was, of course, familiar with Isaiah's account, but he didn't arrive at his account of the City by merely rewriting Isaiah 60. Both Isaiah and John—or so I believe—actually had glimpses of the City which is to come. They "saw" the same City, received revelations from the same God.

While their accounts are strikingly similar, they differ in focus. John speaks in general terms of "the glory and the honor of the nations," while Isaiah describes the processional in considerable detail, identifying animals and vessels and commercial goods. John is more interested than Isaiah is in the glittering "hardware" and the architectural details of the City—offering, as Isaiah does not, an inventory of jewels and a list of numerical measurements. But Isaiah focuses more clearly on the moving figures, human and animal, which walk the City's streets.

Both writers seem to be impressed by the dazzling light of the City. They observe a new Jerusalem which is thoroughly illuminated. The City's light is magnetic; the people and things which are gathered into the City seem to be "pulled" there by the irresistible force of its illumination.

Isaiah's account of his vision opens with a joyful announcement concerning the illumination of the City: "Arise, shine; for your light has come" (Isa. 60:1). He seems to greet this light as something long-awaited. Think of the difference between "There is a package for you" and "Your package has come." The former is simply an announcement, whereas the latter presupposes anticipation, longing. And so it is with the light which illuminates the City.

The light which comes to the City has banished the darkness, the spread of evil and fear which has been permitted under the judgment of God: "behold, darkness and distress; and the light is darkened by its clouds" (Isa. 5:30); "behold, distress and darkness, the gloom of anguish; and they will be thrust into thick darkness" (Isa. 8:22); "for behold, darkness shall cover the earth, and thick darkness the peoples" (Isa. 60:2).

It is not possible for us to empathize fully with the ancient people's fear of the darkness. We live in a technologically illuminated world—it is "always daytime," we are told, in Las Vegas and Monte Carlo. But in earlier times darkness was a phenomenon to be struggled with daily because the technology of extensive illumination was not available. Dwelling places were less secure. And beasts and enemies lurked in the darkness—a population of hostile forces which was in turn greatly expanded by ancient mythology.

But we can draw on examples from our own limited experience to muster at least a partial empathy for this dread of the darkness: our memories of being banished to darkened rooms when we misbehaved as children, of brief periods of electronic "blackouts," of the camping trip where illumination was something to be groped after clumsily in a dark tent at 3:00 A.M. By recalling such experiences or by using our imaginations, we can perhaps share in Isaiah's joy as he greets the light of the dawn which has come to the City of Zion—a dawn to which the citizens of the City must be aroused from their slumbers: "Arise, shine; for your light has come."

What is the *power* which illuminates the City that Isaiah envisions? It is "the glory of the Lord" which has risen upon the City (v. 1). Throughout the Bible the glory of God's presence is regularly associated with illumination. To note only a few examples: God speaks to Moses from a flaming bush; the children of Israel are led by "a pillar of fire to give them light"; the light of the glory of the Lord shines round about the shepherds on the night of Jesus' birth; and Saul of Tarsus is blinded by the light on the road to Damascus.

And here in the transformed City the light of God's glory is pervasive, a never-ending illumination:

> The sun shall be no more your light by day,
> nor for brightness shall the moon
> give light to you by night;
> but the Lord will be your everlasting light,
> and your God will be your glory.
> Your sun shall no more go down,
> nor your moon withdraw itself;
> for the Lord will be your everlasting light,
> and your days of mourning shall be ended. (Isa. 60:19-20)

But in John's account of the transformed City we gain an important piece of information, something not found in Isaiah's prophecy. The key fact which John reveals is that *Jesus* is the source of the City's light: "And the city has no need of sun or moon to shine upon it, for the glory of God is its light, and its lamp is the Lamb" (Rev. 21:23). It is difficult to believe that John is not consciously expanding on Isaiah's account here. He repeats Isaiah's insistence that sun and moon will not be necessary in the City. He too describes the light of the City as that of "the glory of God." But he adds this one significant fact, which in a single stroke takes us far beyond anything that Isaiah might have envisioned: "its lamp is the Lamb."

To those who have come upon this announcement by reading their way through the New Testament record, this will not, of course, be a completely novel piece of information. Already in John's Gospel we learn that Jesus is "the true light that enlightens every man," the light that "shines in the darkness, and the darkness has not overcome it" (John 1:5, 9). " 'I am the light of the world,' " Jesus said during his earthly ministry; " 'he who follows me will not walk in darkness, but will have the light of life' " (John 8:12). As we read through the pages of the New Testament, then, we become aware of the fact that Jesus is a unique source of divine light—aware of it long before we arrive at this announcement in the final chapters of the Book of Revelation.

But if we allow Isaiah 60 and Revelation 21 and 22 to stand side by side, ignoring for present purposes the four hundred pages of Scripture which separate them, John's additional item of information is a startling one. Isaiah is impressed by the City's dazzling light, but when he turns directly to its source, his vision seems to become clouded. He sees no distinct shape at the center of the light's source; he is aware only of the dazzling, pervasive presence of the glory of the Lord. But John's attention focuses clearly on the center of illumination. He sees a discernible figure standing at that point where the light shines most brightly, and he cries out in recognition: "its lamp is the Lamb!"

That Jesus, the Lamb of God, will stand in the center of the transformed City is no minor detail. It is a very central fact about the nature of the City which God has prepared. The City envisioned here is magnetic—more accurately, it is the *light* of the City which is attracting all that is included in the procession into the City: "nations shall come to your light, and kings to the brightness of your rising" (Isa. 60:3). And now, because of what John tells us about the source of the City's light, we can be even more specific: Jesus is the power that attracts the procession into the City.

" 'And I, when I am lifted up from the earth, will draw all men to myself.' He said this to show by what death he was to die" (John 12:32-33). As the eternal Word, Jesus has always been the true light. But in a profound sense, hinted at many times in the New Testament, his illuminatory power, his "attractiveness" as the light of the world, has been "added to" by his redemptive work as the Lamb of God who was lifted up as a sacrifice at Golgotha. In his moving description of the drama of redemption in Philippians 2, Paul links the "humiliation" and the "exaltation" of Jesus with a bold "therefore"—*because* Jesus humbled himself, taking human shape in an obedience which led to the Cross, "*therefore* God has highly exalted him," bestowing a title upon him that will some day bring all rulers to bow at his feet (vv. 5-11).

The redemptive ministry which Jesus accomplished by his life, death, and resurrection constitutes a crucial transaction which has added something to the power, the authority, and—as it were—the illuminative attractiveness of the Son of God. It is Jesus, the eternal divine Logos, whose light fills the City.

But in an important and profound sense, it is also Jesus as the *Lamb* who functions here as the lamp of God's glory. He illuminates the City as the one who has been lifted up on the Cross, and who now gathers all authority and power into his own person.

There is an underlying pattern here, one which we have already noticed in more specific contexts: God takes historical development seriously. Just as the City is, in a sense, the Garden-plus-the-"filling," so the Lamb is the Logos-plus-the-Cross. Because the City contains more than the Garden did, the light of God's victory in the end time—the illuminative power of the Lamb—must include more than the glory that filled the original, unfallen creation. The fact of sin brought about a state of affairs which required a transaction that would go beyond the original work of creation. From the very beginning Jesus was the Logos, by whom all things were made. But because of sinful historical developments the divine Word also had to become the Lamb of God. Sin required that Jesus be the one on whom there was "*bestowed* . . . the name which is above every name."

And so it is the Lamb who is the lamp of the City that will appear at the end of human history. In recent years this profound truth has been denied from two different directions. It is one of the sad and puzzling facts about recent understandings of the person and work of Jesus Christ that those who profess a "high Christology" have seemed to care very little about a critical perspective on cultural patterns, and that those in the Christian community who have been very concerned about cultural issues have often operated with a "low Christology." The important error in each of these cases has to do with a failure to comprehend the implications of the fact that the Lamb is the lamp of the City.

This fact, then, must first of all be pointed to for the benefit of those who have professed to honor Jesus as the Lamb of God but who have paid little attention to the cultural dimensions of his atoning work. Some Christians have greatly emphasized the *individual* benefits of the redemptive ministry of Jesus Christ. They have viewed the work of the Cross almost exclusively in terms of a transaction that took place to effect the salvation of individuals:

> My sin—O the bliss of this glorious thought!—
> My sin, not in part, but the whole,
> Is nailed to the cross, and I bear it no more;
> Praise the Lord, it is well with my soul.

We ought not to belittle this important emphasis in any way. It is an emphasis that has come to be associated with an "evangelical" type of faith; indeed, it expresses something of the very heart of the Protestant Reformation. Jesus died to cancel the debt of our individual sins, and the believer is justified by faith in this atoning sacrifice. Every person who trusts in Jesus as the one who has "paid it all" can live in the confidence that he or she has been granted an everlasting pardon from the penalty of sin. The saved individual has every reason to cry out in joy and confidence, "It is forevermore well with my soul!"

The love of God which has reached humankind in a special way in the redemptive work of Jesus is an "individualizing" love, addressed to unique persons. The salvation of one-of-a-kind men and women is an important element in the atoning work of the Lamb of God. *Names* will be written in the Lamb's Book of Life.

Some Christians have expressed suspicions about this emphasis on the salvation of individuals; some have even ridiculed those who have insisted that this is a central emphasis in the Gospel. They have feared that a strong pattern of "individualism" lurks just beneath the surface of "I-centered" expressions of Christian faith.

We cannot deny that dangerous tendencies manifest themselves in this kind of piety. But a fear that the truth might be distorted must not lead us to relax our grip on the truth. As James Cone has pointed out in his important book, *The Spirituals and the Blues*, the pronoun "I" had an important place in the piety of the black slaves in North America. But as Professor Cone also argues, it would be wrong to dismiss this piety as mere "individualism." The Christian slave in North America suffered from a degradation that is extremely difficult for many of us to imagine—a degradation resulting from a yoke that was forged by racist and imperialist forces which conspired to destroy the unique personhood of the black slave. But these attempts at destruction consistently failed—and the failure was never more obvious than when the forces of oppression encountered a slave who had appropriated the claims of the Gospel in a personal way.

The Christian slave was able to withstand the onslaught of dehumanizing forces because of a trust in the liberating work of the Lamb of God. Stripped of all family and other communal bonds, rendered nameless by a system that treated the slave as a piece of flesh to be bought and sold at the whim of the oppressor, the slave took refuge in a relationship which all of the combined forces of hell could not destroy. As the black "spiritual" describes this relationship: "Look what a wonder that Jesus has done/King Jesus has died for me."

There is nothing that is intrinsically inappropriate, then, about an understanding of the Gospel which strongly emphasizes the individualizing love of God. Indeed, properly understood, this emphasis can express a profound comprehension of the Gospel.

The dangers arise when this element is emphasized to the exclusion of other important dimensions of the work of the Lamb. Jesus died to save sinners—but he is also the Lamb who serves as the lamp in the transformed City. As the Lamb of God he will draw all of the goods, artifacts, and instruments of culture to himself; the kings of the earth will return their authority and power to the Lamb who sits upon the throne; Jesus is the one whose blood has purchased a multi-national community, composed of people from every tribe and tongue and nation. His redemptive ministry, *as* the ministry of the Lamb, is cosmic in scope.

Similar matters must be stressed for the sake of those who want a culturally "relevant" Christianity that is not based on the solid foundation of a full biblical Christology. Here too, of course, we must concede many of the basic concerns at work in this pattern of thinking. Jesus came to rescue a creation which was pervasively infected by the curse of sin—an infection not limited to the psychic territory populated by "human hearts." The curse of sin touches the natural realm, reaching into art and economics, affecting family relationships and educational endeavors, holding thrones and budgets in its grip.

The Bible does present us with a "social gospel." It does link "Christ and culture," proclaiming a message about "the liberation of structures." Sin may have originated in the rebellious designs of individual wills, but human rebellion has *institutionalized* sin. Wickedness has become "codified"; evil has become a part of the very fabric of human sociality. "Changed hearts" will *not* "change society" if the efforts at change are not also directed toward the structures and patterns of human interaction.

The work of the Cross is a many-faceted transaction. There are, in a sense, several "theologies of atonement" hinted at in the Scriptures. The Cross was a transaction between the first and second Persons of the Trinity, wherein the Son offered himself to the Father as a substitutionary sacrifice, a "ransom for sin." And on the Cross Jesus encountered the principalities and powers, defeating them in spite of the fury they expended in their effort to destroy him. The dying Jesus also provides us with a profound display of "selfless love."

It would be wrong, then, to limit our descriptions of Jesus' ministry to one set of categories when the Bible itself employs a rich variety of images and concepts. But it would also be wrong to ignore one of the significant strands of the Bible's portrayal of the work of the Cross. Thus, whatever else we might be compelled to say about the atoning work of Christ, this element must not be denied: Jesus shed his blood to rescue the creation from the curse of sin. And the cleansing blood of Christ must reach not only into the hearts and lives of individuals, but into every corner of the creation which the curse has affected.

I noted earlier the evangelical declaration that "it is well with my soul," and insisted that this is an important and profoundly biblical expression of Christian assurance. But it is not enough. It is a *central* confession, but it is *a* central confession; it is not a full expression of Christian assurance. The God who declares here and now that it is "well" with my soul is the same creating Lord who once looked at the whole world which he had made and proclaimed, "This is good." This God wants once again to say that things are "well" with his entire creation—and he will someday do so when he announces:

'' 'Behold, I make all things new . . . It is done! I am the Alpha and Omega, the beginning and the end' '' (Rev. 21:5-6). ''It is well with my soul'' is only a first step, an initial fruit of God's redeeming activity. We must share in God's restless yearning for the renewal of the cosmos.

Evangelical Protestants have rightly emphasized the ''transactional'' dimensions of the atoning work of Christ over against the teaching of the theological liberals. But in their own ways evangelicals too have operated with a restricted view of the redemptive ministry of Jesus. They have placed limits on the scope and power of the Cross. In boasting of a ''full Gospel'' they have often proclaimed a truncated Christianity. In speaking of a blood which cleanses from all unrighteousness, they have consistently restricted the meaning of the word ''all.'' The problem might be described in this way: they have given *full* reign to the blood of Christ within a *limited* area. They have seen the work of Christ as being a totally transforming power only within individual lives. They have not shown much interest in the work of the Lamb as it applies to the broad reaches of culture or the patterns of political life, nor as a power that heals the racism, ethnocentrism, sexism, and injustice which have for so long poisoned human relationships. To such Christians we must insist that the Lamb is indeed the lamp of the City; just as we must insist to liberal Christians that the light which illuminates the City does indeed issue from the Lamb who shed his own blood as a ransom for sin.

In his classic book *Christ and Culture*, H. Richard Niebuhr utilized a definition of ''culture'' which was common among social scientists during the period in which he was writing. Culture, Niebuhr suggested, should be understood as ''the 'artificial, secondary environment' which man superimposes on the natural. It comprises language, habits, ideas, beliefs, customs, social organization, inherited artifacts, technical processes, and values.''

This is helpful for our present purposes. In the creation account of Genesis 1, God creates two components of what we might think of as the ''primary environment of the creation'': non-human nature, the animals and plants; and human nature, the man and woman whom God created in his own image. As previously noted, God then tells these humans to ''fill'' the earth in obedience to his will. The ''filling'' referred to here contains at least an implicit reference to the creation of the "artificial, secondary environment" mentioned by Niebuhr. In forming the artifacts and instruments and institutions of culture, human beings have added to the population of the original creation.

In an important sense, then, the "world," the *cosmos*, which Jesus came to save was bigger than the world which he originally created. Not only did this world contain many more people than had populated the original Garden, but it was filled with the languages, habits, ideas, beliefs, customs, social organizations, inherited artifacts, technical processes, and values to which Niebuhr refers. And these items were and are touched by human rebellion. They comprise *sinful* culture. But they do belong to the fullness of the cosmos for which Christ died; "for God sent the Son into the cosmos, not to condemn the cosmos, but that the cosmos might be saved through him" (John 3:17).

Already in his earthly ministry Jesus showed something of his power as the Lord over all nature and culture. He demonstrated his control over winds and waves, over disease and death. He most certainly challenged existing habits, ideas, beliefs, customs, and values. And in both subtle and obvious ways he confronted the existing patterns of commerce, politics, and ethnicity.

The often subtle and always partial work that Jesus performed during his earthly ministry will someday be publicly completed in the midst of the transformed City. His Lordship over the whole cosmos must someday be made visible, must be openly vindicated. The authority of the Lamb must be made obvious to the entire creation.

The Lamb is the lamp of the City who will draw all of the works of culture, and all rulers and peoples, to himself. He will do so, first of all, as the true *source* to whom all things and peoples will return. "All things were made through him, and without him was not anything made that was made" (John 1:3); "For in him all things were created, in heaven and on earth, visible and invisible, whether thrones or dominions or principalities or authorities—all things were created through him and for him" (Col. 1:16). Jesus is the one who has been, from the very beginning, "upholding the universe by his word of power" (Heb. 1:3).

But, secondly, Jesus is the *judge* over the "filling" of the earth. In his light all of the products and peoples and rulers will be exposed for what they are. The Lamb will seek out and illuminate the secret patterns of sinful history. In his presence the proud and haughty will be brought low. All knees will bow before him in humble submission.

And, thirdly, he will be the *healer* of the cultures and nations and peoples of the earth. Art and commerce and politics and race relations will experience the cleansing and sanctifying power of the Cross. John tells us that in the City God himself "will wipe away every tear from their eyes . . . neither shall there be mourning nor crying nor pain any more, for the former things have passed away" (Rev. 21:4). We have often employed this theme as a set of sentiments to apply to very "personal" kinds of suffering. The tears which are shed over the loss of a loved one will be wiped away; the pain of cancer and the crying of the physically disabled will be eliminated.

True enough; we have rightly appealed to such sentiments to comfort ourselves in trying situations. But this theme also applies to more "corporate" matters. The tears of the oppressed peoples of human history will be wiped away, as the former captives lead their former captors into the City. The mourning of the poor and the cries of the widow and the orphan will be silenced. The pain of torture and imprisonment will be eliminated. The Lamb's light will chase away the shadows which have hung like a weight over racist and patriarchal societies; it will forever banish the darkness that has permeated the ghettos and barrios and reservations and concentration camps. The transformed City will be ruled by peace and righteousness, and salvation and praise will be emblazoned on its walls.

The Lamb is the lamp of the City. Abraham Kuyper once expressed the general point here in a helpful way: "There is not one inch in the entire area of our human life about which Christ, who is Sovereign of all, does not cry out, 'Mine!' " Many people, of course, would scoff at this way of putting the case. The Marxist would insist that by picturing Jesus as "the supreme property-owner" we are projecting the concept of "possession" into our most ultimate account of the nature of reality. On the other hand, many defenders of "private property" would resist the suggestion that there is, in the final analysis, only one "owner" of reality.

We must not allow these reactions to intimidate us into relinquishing the hope that the Son of God will gather all things unto himself in the end time. The sacrifice of the Lamb of God is indeed a redeeming—a re-purchasing—of that which has been held in the grip of sin. Because of the Cross, God's ownership-relationship to his creation has been restored. But Jesus is not a feudal lord nor a capitalist entrepreneur. When he cries out "Mine!" his tone is not that of the child whose favorite toy has been taken away. Jesus gathers the rebellious creation to himself not because he selfishly desires to assert himself or to seek his own "profit," but because he longs to heal that which has been severely wounded by the ravages of sin.

The fact that the Lamb will be the lamp of the Eternal City has profound implications for the very practical ways in which we are to live in the present age. But it is also important to notice that whenever Jesus is portrayed as the victorious Lamb in the Book of Revelation, the immediate response evoked is that of worship. The heavenly citizens bow low when the Lamb appears—or they break forth into songs of adoration. John himself is so overwhelmed by his vision of the Holy City and of the Lamb that he immediately falls down to worship the angel who showed him these things (Rev. 22:8-9)—an episode which injects an almost humorous portrayal of human awkwardness into the very last passage of the Bible.

However misdirected they may be, John's instincts here are legitimate. Our response to these visions of the Heavenly City will be woefully inadequate if they do not bring us to our knees in worship and honor of the Lamb of God, before whose light all other sources of illumination grow dim:

Fair is the sunshine, Fair is the moonlight,
Bright the sparkling stars on high;
Jesus shines brighter, Jesus shines purer
Than all the angels in the sky.

Fairest Lord Jesus!

Seeking the Celestial City

"For here we have no lasting city,
but we seek the city which is to come" (Heb. 13:14).

Thus the writer to the Hebrews succinctly expresses the practical implications of the Bible's portrayal of the Holy City. But taken by itself this summary is *too* succinct. It is compatible with widely divergent proposals concerning how we ought to live here and now.

One such proposal is that spelled out in John Bunyan's classic *The Pilgrim's Progress.* The spiritual attitudes of many generations of Christians have been affected by this powerful portrayal of the Christian pilgrim's journey from the City of Destruction to the Celestial City. The central character in Bunyan's allegorical tale is given the name "Christian." Having been pointed in the direction of the Good City by Evangelist, Christian sets out on his pilgrimage toward the Gates of Light. Along the way he encounters many dangers and temptations, but he is carried along on his journey by his heartfelt desire to walk the streets of the Celestial City.

Bunyan portrays the Christian life as a very "individual" affair. Christian is often alone in his struggles with the beasts and monsters and human detractors he meets along the way, aided only by his sword or by a well-chosen pious phrase. True, sometimes he is rescued by the likes of Piety and Charity and Hope; but these "companions" represent very personal qualities of heart and mind.

Those of us who have drawn much spiritual nourishment from Bunyan's portrayal of the Christian pilgrimage will be reluctant simply to dismiss his perspective as misguided. We can learn much from Bunyan in our attempts to understand what he calls "the race of saints, in this our gospel day." The

dangers and temptations which he describes so graphically are
very real features of the Christian pilgrimage. What Christian
has not on occasion taken a lonely walk through the Slough
of Despond? And who of us can claim to be unfamiliar with
the temptations posed in the words of a Mr. Worldly Wiseman
or a Mr. Money-Love?

Bunyan's account of the Christian pilgrimage is not so
much false, then, as it is incomplete. And when this partial
picture of the Christian sojourn is taken as the comprehensive
one—as it has been by so many Christians—the result can be
a very myopic brand of Christianity. When the Christian life
as such is viewed as a-lonely-journey-through-a-hostile-world,
it is difficult to find a context for thinking about economic injustice or racial discrimination. Bunyan seems to have very little
awareness of those sins which beset us as communal beings;
his wandering pilgrim travels through a world which appar-
ently knows nothing of slavery or colonialism or militarism.

It is easy for those of us who care about the "corporate"
dimensions of human life to criticize effectively the narrowness
of a Bunyanesque pietism. But there are at least two reasons
why we ought to curb our critical instincts here. First, as has
already been suggested, much in the pietist version of the
Christian life is commendable. It may be that Bunyan and his
cohorts tell only part of the story—but it is an important part.
Second, if the pietist perspective has its defects, so do those
perspectives which have been offered as alternatives to pietism.
Indeed, many of the "horizontalist" systems which have arisen
in reaction to the defects of pietistic "verticalism" have proved
inadequate precisely because they have failed to ground their
vision of the Christian life where Bunyan does—in the individual's acceptance of God's preserving mercies.

It is most fruitful—or so it seems to me—to begin where
Bunyan begins, building and expanding upon the fundamental commitments to which he gives profound expression. For
example, at one point in his story Bunyan has Faith instruct
Christian to seek that kind of holiness which is attained "not
by talk only, as a hypocrite or a talkative person may do, but
by a practical subjection, in faith and love, to the power of the
Word." And later on Mr. Stand-fast, who is about to be trans-
lated into the glorified state, testifies that "I have loved to hear

my Lord spoken of, and wherever I have seen the print of his shoe in the earth, there I have coveted to set my foot too."

These are powerful expressions of a Christian piety whose implications are, in the best sense of the word, "radical." In constructing a proper foundation for "Christian social action" or "political witness" or "cultural involvement," we would be hard-pressed to find a better place to begin. Pious Christians are not to be faulted for insisting on the need for "a practical subjection to the power of the Word," or for desiring to follow the footprints of Jesus. Rather, they must be challenged—and we along with them—to reflect carefully on the implications of these sentiments.

Pious talk about "the power of the Word" and the "print" of Jesus is a very important formal acknowledgment of the authority of Christ and his Word. Once that acknowledgment is recorded, however, it is crucial to turn to the substantive questions. What does the Word *teach*? For what tasks does it empower us when we offer it our "practical subjection"? Into what kinds of activities do the footprints of Jesus lead us?

Recently I heard a very pious man say, "I don't mean to suggest that it is wrong to pay attention to some of these social issues—but I do wish we would spend more time talking about the things of the Lord!" There was no need to attack his fundamental premise. Of course it is of the utmost importance that we talk about the things of the Lord. But the important question is this: What are the Lord's "things"? Doesn't Jesus agonize over attacks on the dignity of those persons for whom he spilled his blood? Doesn't he grieve over men and women who have been imprisoned because they witnessed for justice and righteousness? Isn't the Son of God angered by the oppression of widows and orphans, and by the schemes of those who plot the destruction of all that the creator has called "good"? If so, then many so-called "social issues" *are* "the things of the Lord."

Indeed, this exploration of the visions of the Holy City recorded in Isaiah and Revelation is intended to show that "the things of the Lord" extend across a very wide territory. The ships of Tarshish and the cedars of Lebanon—whatever their perverse uses in the present age—belong to the Lord. The Lord continues to lay claim to the political structures of human societies. And he will not allow the present racial, ethnic, and linguistic divisions of humankind to hinder his work of human reclamation. "The earth is the Lord's and the fulness thereof, the world and those who dwell therein."

All of this must be kept in mind as we "seek the city which is to come." And we must allow these visions of the Celestial City to shape and inform our patterns of seeking.

Most Christians would assent to the instruction given in Hebrews 13:14. As we have seen, Bunyan portrayed his pilgrim as seeking the City. The passengers on the Mayflower also thought of themselves as seekers of the Holy City, and so did those South African trekkers who enslaved their black neighbors. Proponents of the "social gospel," advocates of "liberation theology," shapers of "moral majorities," and builders of Crystal Cathedrals—all of them lay claim to a search for the City which is to come.

But how does the Bible instruct us to seek the City? When, for example, the writer to the Hebrews describes the Christian life as a search for the Holy City, what patterns of living does he have in mind?

The immediate context of Hebrews 13:14 does provide an answer to this question. In verses 11 and 12 of this chapter the writer draws a parallel between the death of Jesus and a practice in the ritual of the Old Testament. On the day of atonement the high priest would carry the blood of animals into the holy of holies—blood which played a key role in the cultic ceremony. But the flesh and bones from which the blood was drawn had no ritualistic status. The animals' bodies were merely carried outside the camp to be burned. Similarly, the writer argues, Jesus' death took place "outside the gate." His death had no place within the cultic ritual of the Jewish religion of his day. From the point of view of that religious system, his body, like the bodies of the animals in the Old Testament, was fit only for the garbage heap.

It would be wrong to push this analogy too far. The writer does not mean to suggest, for example, that since it was misguided for the Jews to have rejected Jesus, it was also misguided for them to have burned the bodies of sacrificial animals in the Old Testament. But the disanalogies are not important. The parallel drawn here is intended to illustrate only one point:

just as the Old Testament animals were destroyed outside of the cultic context, so Jesus—the Lamb of God, the only true and worthy sacrifice for sin—was viewed as irrelevant to the religious system of his day.

Having drawn this analogy, the writer introduces a resolution in verse 13: "Therefore let us go forth to him outside the camp, and bear the abuse he endured." As Christians we are followers of the one who was despised and rejected by his contemporaries, and we must not be afraid to join him in his rejected status. Indeed, we must flee to Jesus, joining him "outside the camp," bearing abuse for him.

It is at this point that the theme of the Holy City is introduced: "For here we have no lasting city, but we seek the city which is to come." In view of our discussion of the Lamb as the lamp of the Holy City, we cannot help but note that once again the theme of the Holy City is linked to the sacrificial work of Christ on the Cross. The Lamb of God is not only the source of illumination for the future City; he is also the illuminator of the path which leads to that City. And the way to the renewed Jerusalem is one along which we must participate in the abuse which Jesus endured. "I shall ne'er catch sight of the gates of light if the way of the Cross I miss."

Christians must expect to suffer abuse, then, as they travel to the City. But the writer to the Hebrews goes on immediately to specify the shape of the Christian sojourn:

> Through him then let us continually offer up a sacrifice of praise to God, that is, the fruit of lips that acknowledge his name. Do not neglect to do good and to share what you have, for such sacrifices are pleasing to God. (vv. 15-16)

Here we encounter a very common theme in the apostolic writings: the call to "do good" or to "perform good works"—an emphasis that we often find when the writers are discussing the Christian's relationship to the social status quo (see, for example, Romans 13 and I Peter 2). This mandate also comes directly from Jesus' lips during his earthly ministry: "Let your light so shine before men, that they may see your good works and give glory to your Father who is in heaven" (Matt. 5:16).

In recent years there has been a revival of interest in some Christian circles in a "theology of the poor." Christians have rediscovered the Bible's portrayal of God as "the God of the oppressed," and of the godly life as one in which we must identify with the concerns of the poor and disadvantaged. This is a concern which the writer to the Hebrews seems to share. The insistence that Christians "do not neglect to do good" is immediately linked to the need to "share what you have, for such sacrifices are pleasing to God." Our journey to the Holy City is one of actively "seeking" the City, which involves our suffering the abuse of identifying with those who are in need.

Examining the immediate context of Isaiah 60 reveals a similar "praxis" emphasis. In the two preceding chapters Isaiah examines the problems of economic and political justice in considerable detail. Isaiah 59 contains a lengthy description of a society in which "justice is far from us, and righteousness does not overtake us" (v. 9). But the people of God should have nothing to do with these patterns. Rather, "if you pour yourself out for the hungry and satisfy the desire of the afflicted, then shall your light rise in the darkness and your gloom be as the noonday" (Isa. 58:10). The light of God's glory, which bursts forth in everlasting brilliance in the Holy City of chapter 60, can be partially realized in the midst of an unjust society. And according to Isaiah it is realized along lines which are similar to the instruction in Hebrews 13 "to share what you have": God's people must, Isaiah says, pour themselves out on behalf of the afflicted.

And it is no accident that chapter 60, with its profound portrayal of the Holy City, should be immediately followed by one of the great "liberation" announcements of the Bible, a passage which the Lord Jesus himself chose (see Luke 4:16-19) as the inaugural text for his own ministry:

> The Spirit of the Lord is upon me,
> because the Lord has anointed me
> to bring good tidings to the afflicted;
> he has sent me to bind up the brokenhearted,
> to proclaim liberty to the captives,
> and the opening of the prison to those who are bound.
> (Isa. 61:1)

In the opening pages of this book I said that if I had to choose under pressure I would identify myself with the "Christ transforming culture" camp. But I also said that I would want to qualify this identification in important ways. It may be helpful here, in the concluding pages of my discussion, to explore these qualifications.

The transformationalist camp is correct, as I view things, in *expecting* the transformation of culture. Much of what I have said in this book is offered to support this contention. Christ *will* transform culture at the end time. The ships of Tarshish, presently vessels which serve rebellious designs, will someday carry the wealth of the nations into the presence of the Creator. Political power will be gathered into that City wherein the saints will rule forever. The peoples and tribes and nations of the earth will sing praises to the Lamb who was slain. In short, the "filling" of the earth will be harnessed and remolded for the sake of God's glory.

Human culture will *someday* be transformed. Does this mean, then, that we must begin that process of transformation here and now? Are we as Christians called to transform culture in the present age? Not, I think, in any grandiose or triumphalistic manner. We are called to *await* the coming transformation. But we should wait actively, not passively. We must *seek* the City which is to come.

Many activities are proper to this "seeking" life. We can call human institutions to obedience to the Creator. When we invite the manufacturers of weapons to devote themselves to making instruments of peace, we are seeking the City in whose midst swords will be beaten into plowshares. When we propose programs of racial justice, we are actively preparing for the day when the new song to the Lamb will fill the earth. And in a very special and profound way, we prepare for life in the City when we work actively to bring about healing and obedience within the community of the people of God.

The fact is—as we have seen—that the Bible links its portrayals of the Holy City to very practical commands: pour out your lives for the afflicted; comfort the brokenhearted; love your brothers and sisters; feed the hungry. By doing these things here and now, we can experience something of the light of God's glory—a light which will someday shine eternally in the Holy City:

> . . . the darkness is passing away and the true light is already shining. He who says he is in the light and hates his brother is in the darkness still. He who loves his brother abides in the light, and in it there is no cause for stumbling. (I John 2:8-10)

While the Bible does teach—or so I believe—that Christ will transform culture in the end time, there is no clear biblical command to Christians to "transform culture" in any general way. It may be, of course, that what the Bible does tell us to do can be properly construed as a command to transform our present culture. But as we debate such matters we must never lose sight of what the Bible does command us to do in clear and specific terms: "Pour yourself out for the hungry, and satisfy the desire of the afflicted." Whatever our theoretical formulations regarding "Christ and culture," we cannot avoid the clear mandate of the Scriptures. We must actively seek the City by suffering abuse outside the camp.

Of course there is also a passive dimension to our search for the Celestial City. We must allow the light of God's glory to flood our souls, to radiate its warmth there, to bring illumination and healing to the dark places of our own lives. It is only by passively receiving the light of Jesus that we can be active reflectors of that light. In humble submission to the Lord's commandments we can be empowered for those good deeds that will show forth the light of God's peace and justice in a world of oppression and suffering.

These good deeds must be undergirded by the conviction that the earth is indeed the Lord's, and the fullness thereof. The ships of Tarshish will sail into the City's harbor. The rulers of this present age will be called into the presence of the Lamb to submit to his authority. People from many tribes and nations will join in singing the new song of redemption.

Our conviction—our sure hope—that the Lord will bring these things to pass in his own time should lead us to express our discipleship boldly. Our present efforts as citizens of Zion

will culminate in the final victory of the Lamb whose light will
fill the City:

Hark! those bursts of acclamation!
Hark! those loud triumphant chords!
Jesus takes the highest station;
O what joy the sight affords!
Crown Him! Crown Him!
King of Kings, and Lord of Lords.